Extraordinary Jobs with

ANIMALS

Also in the Extraordinary Jobs series:

Extraordinary Jobs for Adventurers
Extraordinary Jobs in Agriculture and Nature
Extraordinary Jobs for Creative People
Extraordinary Jobs in Entertainment
Extraordinary Jobs in the Food Industry
Extraordinary Jobs in Government
Extraordinary Jobs in Health and Science
Extraordinary Jobs in Leisure
Extraordinary Jobs in Media
Extraordinary Jobs in the Service Sector
Extraordinary Jobs in Sports

Extraordinary Jobs with

ANIMALS

ALECIA T. DEVANTIER & CAROL A. TURKINGTON

Ferguson

An imprint of Infobase Publishing

Extraordinary Jobs with Animals

Copyright © 2007 by Alecia T. Devantier and Carol A. Turkington

Ferguson
An imprint of Infobase Publishing
132 West 31st Street
New York NY 10001

ISBN-10: 0-8160-5862-8
ISBN-13: 978-0-8160-5862-4

Library of Congress Cataloging-in-Publication Data

Devantier, Alecia T.
  Extraordinary jobs with Animals / Alecia T. Devantier and Carol A. Turkington.
    p. cm.—(Extraordinary jobs)
  Includes bibliographical references and index.
  ISBN 0-8160-5862-8 (hc: alk. paper)
1. Animal specialists—Vocational guidance—Juvenile literature. I. Turkington, Carol. II. Title. IIII Series: Devantier, Alecia T. Extraordinary jobs.
  SF80.D48 2006
  636.0023—dc 22   2006011382

Ferguson books are available at special discounts when purchased in bulk quantities for businesses, associations, institutions, or sales promotions. Please call our Special Sales Department in New York at (212) 967-8800 or (800) 322-8755.

You can find Ferguson on the World Wide Web at http://www.fergpubco.com

Text design by Mary Susan Ryan-Flynn
Cover design by Salvatore Luongo

Printed in the United States of America

VB MSRF 10 9 8 7 6 5 4 3 2

This book is printed on acid-free paper.

CONTENTS

Acknowledgments vi
Are You Cut Out for a Career with
   Animals? vii
How to Use This Book ix

Animal Behaviorist 1
Animal Forensic Specialist 5
Animal Shelter Director 9
Animal Wrangler 12
Aquarist 17
Assistance Dog Trainer 19
Dog Day Care Owner 23
Dog Groomer 28
Dog Handler 32
Dog Show Judge 36
Dude Rancher 41
Equine Dentist 44
Exotic Animal Veterinarian 47
Farrier 51
Gourmet Dog Treat Baker 56

Holistic Veterinarian 59
Horse Whisperer 64
Marine Mammal Trainer 67
Musher 70
Pet Cemetery Owner 73
Pet Lawyer 76
Pet Photographer 79
Pet Psychic 82
Pet Psychologist 85
Pet Sitter 88
Petting Zoo Operator 92
Pet Waste Removal Specialist 95
Sheep Shearer 99
Wildlife Rehabilitator 102
Zookeeper 105

Appendix A. Associations,
   Organizations, and Web Sites . . 109
Appendix B. Online Career
   Resources 129
Read More About It 137
Index 143

ACKNOWLEDGMENTS

This book wouldn't have been possible without the help of countless others who referred us to individuals to interview and who came up with information about a wide variety of odd and unusual jobs with animals. We deeply appreciate the time and generosity of all those individuals who took the time to talk to us about their unusual jobs with animals.

Thanks also to all the people who helped with interviews and information and the production of this book, including Susan Shelly McGovern, Wanda Miller, and Barbara Turkington.

Thanks also to our editors James Chambers and Sarah Fogarty, to Vanessa Nittoli, and to our agents Ed Claflin and Gene Brissie.

ARE YOU CUT OUT FOR A CAREER WITH ANIMALS?

As a child, were you the one who dragged home the lost kitten, the abandoned puppy on a string, the box turtle, the wren with a broken wing? Did you play "animal hospital" with all of your stuffed animals and family pets in various states of bandages? Did you dream of owning a pony or riding elephants?

If you love animals, you may have thought about working as a vet or an animal trainer. But there are so many more careers out there beyond the obvious that many kids never even consider. If you have a yen to work with or help animals in some way, you might want to consider this field. If you're going to work with animals, you'll need patience, warmth, and respect for all living things. It may also mean you've got to take classes that don't exactly thrill you, but which are necessary just the same.

First of all, ask yourself: *What am I passionate about?* Do you spend every waking moment thinking and dreaming about horses, cats, snakes, or wild animals? Have you always been fascinated with the way dolphins communicate, ever since you stumbled across that first episode of *Flipper*? Do you love the idea of helping sick and injured animals, but you're drawn more to the alternative end of medicine?

If you follow your heart, you're almost guaranteed to find a career working with animals that you'll love. In fact, almost every individual we interviewed for this book repeated the same litany—*I love animals, and I love my job. It's different. It's unusual. It's unique.*

Many unusual jobs in the animal field are every bit as difficult and require just as much training as the more typical, traditional careers. What these more unusual jobs offer, however, is something much harder to measure—and that's a job that lets your spirit soar and allows you to do what you love to do.

Of course, loving what you do is only part of having a successful career working with animals. You've also got to be good at what you want to do. Most of these jobs are so specialized that if you're going to go after one of them, you need to be really good at it and have some really specific training. Whether you're thinking of becoming a blacksmith or a horse whisperer, you need to have the talent and the training to do that job better than most other people.

Then there's the rest of the world. Chances are, if you're like most of us, you've inherited a bevy of *shoulds*. These *shoulds* inside your head can be a major stumbling block in finding and enjoying an unusual career working with animals. Maybe other people won't be so happy with your career choice. You may hear complaints from your family and friends who just can't understand why you don't want a "regular job." They want you to be a doctor, but you may be thinking more about veterinary acupuncture. If you confide your career dreams to some of these folks, they may try to discourage you. Can you handle their continuous skepticism, or downright disappointment? Other people often have their own *shoulds* for you, too.

Or maybe you're having a hard time imagining a different path for yourself because of the obstacles you see. Maybe you're saying to yourself: "There's just no way I can follow my dream and make a living at that. I don't have the right background."

Think again! You can be successful if you don't accept someone else's assessment. If you get bogged down in the belief that you can't follow your dream because of what is, you take away your power to discover what could be. You lose the power to create a different future for yourself.

Almost everyone we've talked to in this book has ended up with an unusual job working with animals by a circuitous route. A few folks have always known exactly what they wanted to do, and did it. But for the rest of us, it can take years to work up the courage to actually do what we knew all along we would have loved to do.

You don't have to start big. You don't have to wake up one day and decide to specialize in veterinary brain surgery. Start with a chemistry class. Check out a couple of books. Try an internship or unconventional summer job. Travel. Volunteer.

Try not to think of learning and working as two totally separate things.

When somebody hands you a diploma, you don't stop learning. School can be the best place to build up your fact-based knowledge—the rest of the things you do provide you with experience-based knowledge. You need both to forge an unusual career working with animals. So take charge of your journey instead of relying on someone else's career path. Take advantage of the things you learn as you plan your next experience.

You may encounter setbacks along the way. How do you handle adversity? How do you feel when you fail? If you've always wanted to work at a racetrack, how will you feel if you have trouble getting a start as a racing stable groom? If no one seems to want to hire you? If you can pick yourself up and keep going, you've probably got the temperament to survive the road to finding an unusual career working with animals.

Learn to look at the world through curious eyes, wherever that takes you. By exploring your options, you'll learn that work and play become the same thing. Push past your doubts and fears—and let your journey begin!

Carol A. Turkington
Alecia T. Devantier

HOW TO USE THIS BOOK

Students face a lot of pressure to decide what they want to be when they grow up. Some kids have discovered their passion right from the beginning: Some just love to work outdoors, planting gardens or building things. Others are fascinated with science, with mathematics, or with languages. But what about those kids who just love furry, finned, or fluttery creatures? Where can you go to learn about these exciting, creative, nontraditional jobs working with animals?

For example, where can you go to find out how to become a farrier? What does it take to become a dog groomer? Is it really possible to make a living as a pet psychic?

Look no further. This book will take you inside the world of a number of different animal-related jobs, answering all sorts of questions you might have, letting you know what to expect if you pursue that career, introducing you to someone making a living that way, and providing resources if you want to do further research.

THE JOB PROFILES

All job profiles in this book have been broken down into the following fact-filled sections: At a Glance, Overview, and Interview. Each offers a distinct perspective on the job, and taken together give you a full view of the job in question.

At a Glance

Each entry starts out with an *At A Glance* box, offering a snapshot of important basic information to give you a quick glimpse of that particular job, including salary, education, requirements, personal attributes, and outlook.

✅ *Salary range.* What can you expect to make? Salary ranges for the jobs in this book are as accurate as possible; many are based on the U.S. Bureau of Labor Statistics' *Occupational Outlook Handbook.* Information also comes from individuals, actual job ads, employers, and experts in that field. It's important to remember that salaries for any particular job vary greatly depending on its geographic location and the level of education and experience required.

✅ *Education/Experience.* What kind of education or experience does the job require? This section will give you some information about the types of education or experience the job might call for.

✅ *Personal attributes.* Do you have what it takes to do this job? How do you think of yourself? How would someone else describe you? This section will give you an idea of some of the personality traits that might be useful in this career. These attributes were collected from articles written about the job, as well as recommendations from employers and people actually doing the jobs, working in the field.

✅ *Requirements.* Are you qualified? You might as well make sure you meet any health, medical, or screening requirements before going any further with your job pursuit.

✅ *Outlook.* What are your chances of finding a job working with animals?

This section is based in part on the *Occupational Outlook Handbook*, as well as on interviews with employers and experts. This information is typically a "best guess" based on the information that is available right now, including changes in the economy, situations in the United States and around the world, job trends and retirement levels, as well as many other factors that can influence changes in the availability of these jobs.

Overview

This section will give you an idea of what to expect from the job. For most of these jobs, there really is no such thing as an average day. Each new day, new job, or new assignment is a whole new adventure, bringing with it a unique set of challenges and rewards. But in general, this section provides a general overview of what a person holding this position might expect on a day-to-day basis.

The overview also gives more details about how to get into the profession. It takes a more detailed look at the required training or education, if needed, giving an in-depth look at what to expect during that training or educational period. If there are no training or education requirements for the job, this section will provide some suggestions for getting the experience you'll need to be successful.

No job is perfect, and the **Pitfalls** section takes a look at some of the obvious and not-so-obvious downsides to the job. In many cases, the number of pitfalls far outweighs the number of perks. Don't let the pitfalls discourage you from pursuing the career; they are just things to be aware of while making your decision.

For many people, loving their job so much that they look forward to going to work every day is enough of a perk. **Perks** looks at some of the other perks of the job you may not have considered.

So what can you do *now* to start working toward the career of your dreams? **Get a Jump on the Job** will give you some ideas and suggestions for things that you can do now, even before graduating from high school, to start preparing for this job. Opportunities include training programs, groups and organizations to join, as well as practical skills to learn.

Interview

In addition to taking a general look at the job, each entry features a discussion with someone who is lucky enough to do this job for a living. In addition to giving you an inside look at the job, the experts offer advice for people wanting to follow in their footsteps, pursuing a career in the same field.

APPENDIXES

Appendix A (Associations, Organizations, and Web Sites) lists places to look for additional information about each specific job, including professional associations, societies, unions, government organizations, Web sites, and periodicals. Associations and other groups are a great source of information, and there's an association for just about every job you can imagine. Many groups and associations have a student membership level, which you can join by paying a small fee. There are many advantages to joining an association, including the chance to make important contacts, receive helpful newsletters, and attend workshops or conferences. Some associations also offer scholarships that will make it easier to further your education. Other sources listed in this section include information about accredited training programs, forums, official government links, and more.

In **Appendix B (Online Career Resources)** we've gathered some of the best general Web sites about unusual jobs with animals. Use these as a springboard to your own Internet research. All of this information was current when this book was written, but Web site addresses do change. If you can't find what you're looking for at a given address, do a simple Web search. The page may have been moved to a different location.

READ MORE ABOUT IT

In this back-of-the-book listing, we've gathered some helpful books that can give you more detailed information about each job we discuss in this book. Find these at the library or bookstore if you want to learn even more about animal-related jobs.

ANIMAL BEHAVIORIST

OVERVIEW

Whether it's teaching an owner how to stop a yellow lab from jumping on company, decoding the behavior of great apes in the wild, taking care of animals in labs or research facilities, or teaching at colleges and universities, all of these jobs are handled by animal behaviorists, whose job it is to study, interpret, and understand the behavior of animals. An animal behaviorist may find him- or herself staying up all night to observe the mating behaviors of frogs, only to have to be in the classroom the next day to teach a group of students. Drug companies and government laboratories hire animal behaviorists to study how drugs, chemicals, or other agents affect an animal's behavior. Other animal behaviorists are hired to train animals to perform. Still others work with assistance animals, spending years studying the most effective ways to prepare a dog to work with the handicapped.

Most scientists involved in animal behavior work in one of four broad fields: anthropology, ethology, behavioral ecology, or comparative psychology, all of which overlap to some degree. In general, ethologists and psychologists are interested in the functions of behavior, while behavioral ecologists specialize in how society and the environment affect behavior. The training of ethologists and behavioral ecologists is usually handled in a department of biology, zoology, ecology and evolution, entomology, wildlife, or other animal science. On the other hand, most

AT A GLANCE

Salary Range

Salaries for animal behaviorists vary tremendously, because the field includes many different kinds of work, and funding comes from a variety of sources. Salaries for animal behaviorists range from about $24,000 to $48,000.

Education/Experience

There are some jobs available to those with bachelor's degrees, but a certified animal behaviorist must have a master's or Ph.D. degree in a behavioral science that meets specific academic requirements. Depending on the certifying organization, a doctorate of veterinary medicine may be required. Many universities offer graduate training programs in animal behavior. For health-related jobs, training in relevant fields such as physiology, biochemistry, or pharmacology will be particularly helpful. For management or consulting jobs, experience in environmental science, conservation biology, or population and community ecology may be useful.

Personal Attributes

You should be inquisitive and genuinely interested in animals and why they behave in the ways that they do. You should be able to work in a methodical manner, be organized and motivated, and be able to work on your own, with limited supervision. Because animal behaviorists who work in the field have to travel to the animals' habitats, it helps to be in good physical condition, as you might find yourself traipsing through jungles or over mountains.

Requirements

Requirements will vary, depending on your employer and the type of work you're doing. In general, research and recording skills are extremely important, since information gathered in the field isn't usable unless it's been recorded and made

(continues)

AT A GLANCE (continued)

available to others. Many animal behaviorists are expected to publish their research as part of their job requirements. Although true animal behaviorists are scholars and many are certified by creditable organizations, there is no license required to use the title or to offer your services.

Outlook

Jobs for animal behaviorists are expected to increase at an average rate through 2012. Although animal behavior is a growing discipline, competition for jobs in teaching and research is very keen.

comparative psychologists are trained in psychology departments. Behaviorists specializing in the study of animal behavior usually study with experts in anthropology, psychology, or sociology.

Animals have always fascinated humans, and the study of animal behavior has been going on since the early 1900s. An animal behaviorist wants to know and understand how animals communicate, their mating habits, their preferences for habitat and food, how they socialize with one another, how they react toward other animals, and much more.

You'll find most animal behaviorists teaching and conducting research in university biology, zoology, or psychology departments. Others work at university departments of animal science, anthropology, ecology, entomology, neuroscience, sociology, or wildlife biology, or in medical or veterinary colleges. Much of the study of animal behavior can be applied to issues affecting humans, as well as animals. Animal behaviorists who have studied the ways in which baby birds develop their song patterns, for instance, have been

able to apply that information to provide unique insights on how human speech development occurs.

To land these jobs, you'll usually need to have a Ph.D., although a few junior colleges may require only a master's. More and more animal behaviorists are being hired by universities to apply behavioral knowledge to the conservation or care of domestic animals, and many work in animal science, veterinary medicine, wildlife conservation, entomology, improving livestock production, managing wildlife populations, or controlling pests.

A few jobs are available at zoos, aquariums, and museums to work as curators or researchers responsible for acquiring, maintaining, and displaying collections of animals. Other animal behaviorists work on research with these animals in captivity.

You'll find more animal behaviorists working in government labs or in the corporate world, often in the field of health-related research, looking at the behavioral effects of new drugs or checking out the link between behavior and disease. Some animal behaviorists help manage wildlife for the government's natural resources programs. Still other behaviorists work as consultants, examining how changing the environment may affect foraging patterns, movement of animals, and animal reproduction.

Pitfalls

You'll need to invest lots of time and money to become an animal behaviorist. Although a limited number of jobs are available to people with a bachelor's degree, most positions require at least a master's degree and preferably a Ph.D. Some jobs require that you be certified as a veterinarian, which means many difficult years of postgraduate work. The number of jobs for animal behaviorists can depend on uncertain funding sources. Government funding, for instance, may be diverted to another area or cut completely, depending on the current economic climate, legislative actions, and other factors.

Perks

The study of animal behavior is fascinating, and you never run out of areas to observe.

The work is usually varied and exciting, with the ever-present possibility of important discoveries and breakthroughs. And you'll get to work in a stimulating environment such as a university or research laboratory with people who share your interests.

Get a Jump on the Job

The most important way you can start preparing now for a career as an animal

Suzanne Hetts, animal behaviorist

If you've got a misbehaving guinea pig, a feisty ferret, or a problem with a companion animal, Suzanne Hetts is the expert to call. Hetts is an animal behaviorist and the co-founder of Animal Behavior Associates, based in Littleton, Colorado. While she focuses mainly on dogs and cats, other animal behaviorists at the company also work with birds, sheep, horses, ferrets, guinea pigs, companion animals, and fish. In addition to working with clients, Hetts sometimes travels for speaking engagements and writes about animal behavior issues.

Armed with an undergraduate degree in medical technology and microbiology, Hetts got her first job as a medical technologist at a large Denver hospital. Her concern for animals and the environment, however, kept tugging at her, and she left her job to pursue a master's degree in wildlife biology. While working as a medical technologist at the Veterinary Teaching Hospital at Colorado State University, she took a class in animal behavior—and got hooked.

She started her business in partnership with a professor while she was still in graduate school. Today, the company offers pet behavior consultations at home, in the company's offices, or via telephone or e-mail to people having problems with their pets. To start with, Hetts works closely with a client so that she can thoroughly understand the pet and its environment, relationship with family members, habits, and behaviors, before beginning the behavioral process. This usually means an extensive interview with the pet owner so Hetts can hear about the animal's daily routines, its history, how the pet behaves in various situations, how the pet relates to family members and others, and the nature and scope of the behavior problem. She also will observe the pet during an office or home consultation.

Once Hetts has a feeling for the animal, the pet owner, and the circumstances, she'll use that information to develop a customized behavior modification plan that could include making changes to the pet's environment or changing the way the owner reacts to the pet's behavior.

Not surprisingly, Hetts and her associates see many of the same basic pet-related problems over and over. The most common include aggression, house soiling, barking, separation anxiety, destructive behavior, and various fears and phobias, all of which can be handled by some basic attention to behavior modification.

"It's very satisfying to be able to help people understand their pets better, improve the pet's quality of life," Hetts says. "Hopefully, [that will] prevent pets from being surrendered to shelters or euthanized due to behavior problems."

behaviorist is to pay close attention to your education. You'll need good grades to get into college, and the best way to get accepted into grad school is to have completed an independent study project or obtained some research experience as an undergraduate. Read everything you can find about animal behavior, and spend as much time with animals as you can. Consider volunteering at an animal shelter, or looking for a job in a pet store, veterinarian's office, or other place where animals are present.

ANIMAL FORENSIC SPECIALIST

OVERVIEW

Picture this: Three cats are discovered dead within a half-mile range. Each of them died from a severe gash to its throat. Rumors are flying and pet owners are keeping their animals in the house, afraid that they'll meet a similar fate. So, how do you solve the mystery and figure out when and how the cats died? Were they killed by a deranged human? Is there a mountain lion on the loose? What's going on?

An animal forensic specialist will be able to tell you.

This relatively new field may involve a variety of tasks. For example, an animal forensic specialist would be called to determine cause of death if a number of domestic animals have been found dead in a particular area. In this case, the local humane association, local government, or an animal rights group might hire an animal forensic specialist to determine if the pets were killed by an animal or a human predator. Prosecution of animal cruelty cases sometimes requires the testimony of an animal forensic specialist, who can determine if an animal was subjected to torture or neglect.

An animal forensic specialist can sometimes tell what has happened to an animal simply by an external examination, but at other times, the specialist may need to conduct a necropsy (an autopsy on an animal). If examinations and necropsies uncover tooth marks (which would indicate the dead animal had been attacked by another animal), the animal forensic specialist would then use

AT A GLANCE

Salary Range

All but a very few animal forensic specialists rely on other jobs—usually in the areas of biology or zoology—to supplement the money they earn conducting forensic work. Someone who practices animal forensics in addition to teaching at a college can expect a combined, beginning salary of about $43,000. Earnings for forensic work may increase as the specialist becomes better known and is asked to handle more jobs.

Education/Experience

You'll need a Ph.D. in biology, zoology, or a related area. Those with bachelor's and master's degrees may be able to get positions in labs, but for research and teaching positions, a Ph.D. will give you a great advantage.

Personal Attributes

You need to have the temperament necessary to work with dead animals. The work can be very unpleasant, so you must have a level of commitment to keep you engaged in the job. You should also have a high level of common sense, and be able to look at a situation from every angle to determine what has occurred.

Requirements

You need an excellent knowledge of animal physiology and animal habits and traits.

Outlook

The field of animal forensics is still fairly new, so the number of jobs may be limited. Poaching violations, the development of state and federal hunting regulations, the Endangered Species Act of 1973, and the United National Convention on International Trade in Endangered Species (CITIES) are some of the factors that helped create this new field.

those tooth marks to try to determine what type of animal was the predator. If no tooth marks can be found, the specialist may need to look further, investigating fur, bones, and *scat* (fecal matter).

Most state environmental departments have animal pathologists on hand, but the pathologists primarily work on cases where animals have died of natural causes, unlike animal forensic specialists, who are called in to investigate questionable deaths.

An animal forensic specialist might be called in to determine if illegal poaching has occurred—anything from a hunter taking game out of season to a poacher harvesting protected mussels. He or she might also assist in cases where endangered species may have been moved illegally from one spot to another.

Wildlife forensic specialists detect illegal trading in wildlife articles such as ivory tusks, lion or tiger skins, bones, furs—even internal organs of animals such as gall bladders—all of which are illegal to bring into the United States. When the only thing a wildlife criminal leaves behind is a bit of blood, a couple of bones, or a few feathers, it's up to the wildlife forensic specialist to track down the solution to the crime.

The U.S. Fish and Wildlife Service owns and operates a forensics laboratory in Ashland, Oregon, where about 30 forensic employees at the laboratory enforce wildlife laws for law enforcement agencies at the federal, state, and international level. This lab was established in 1989 when the government realized that university and museum scientists just couldn't keep up with the caseload. The Ashland lab is staffed by scientists recruited from universities, museums, police departments, and human forensic laboratories. Because the lab was the first of its kind, the field of wildlife forensics was established as cases were referred to Oregon. These forensic specialists provide the casework to support investigations as well as the forensic evidence at trials. This

might include anything from checking out improperly imported evidence (such as fur coats and lizard boots) to identifying exotic animal parts used in international trafficking or smuggling investigations. Although the Ashland laboratory is the only one of its kind in the world, you can find related forensic animal specialist jobs in agencies such as the U.S. Fish and Wildlife Service, National Park Service, and other government agencies.

The identification of wildlife evidence is complicated by the fact that wildlife enforcement officers rarely seize whole animals, which can be readily identified by a museum or zoo expert. Instead, it's far more typical to confiscate parts and products of these animals as evidence, which rarely contains the characteristics that define an animal species. Some of this evidence might include blood on a hunter's clothing; fresh, frozen, or smoked meats; loose hair; fur coats; reptile leather products such as purses, belts, or shoes; loose feathers or down; carved ivory objects; sea turtle oil; shell jewelry; or powdered rhinoceros horn.

In addition, while human forensic specialists must be expert in just one species (*Homo sapiens*), wildlife forensic scientists must be prepared to identify evidence from any species in the world that is illegally killed, smuggled, poached, or sold.

Pitfalls

Funding for animal forensic work is limited, and the work is expensive to conduct. Animal and wildlife forensic jobs are competitive, and most require a high level of education, which means you'll spend a lot of time and money before you can become qualified. The demand for animal forensic work is limited, forcing specialists to do other jobs in addition to forensic work.

Brad Swanson, animal forensic specialist

Brad Swanson has become well known for his animal forensic work, and greatly enjoys the challenges involved. A professor at Central Michigan University in Mount Pleasant, Swanson has been called upon on numerous occasions to determine the causes of mysterious animal deaths. He relies on help from teams of graduate students at the university.

With undergraduate and master's degrees in zoology, and a Ph.D. in biology with an emphasis on ecology and genetics, Swanson is well qualified for animal forensic work. "The skills I picked up while working on my Ph.D. allowed me to be able to do this," Swanson says.

While the work is interesting and important, Swanson warns that it isn't glamorous, and sometimes it can be downright ugly. For example, he recalls one case that involved a number of cats found dead in a suburb north of Seattle. The cats had been found in pieces, with their internal organs removed. "I was having nightmares for weeks," Swanson says. "I have cats and I'm a real cat lover." Because a local teenager had been bragging about killing cats and was being blamed for the deaths, Swanson was determined to find out what had really happened.

"You know, maybe the kid had done it, and then I would have wanted to see him punished as much as anybody," Swanson says. "But if it turned out that he hadn't done it, I wanted to make sure he wasn't blamed unfairly and end up having his life ruined."

A local veterinarian speculated that the cat deaths had been intentional, and had been carried out by humans. When the police sent the cat carcasses to Swanson's lab, however, Swanson was quickly able to determine that another animal was to blame.

"It became obvious from the wounds that a canid [mammals of the family Canidae, which include dogs, wolves, coyotes, jackals, and foxes] had grabbed a hold of the cat," he recalls. "There was a drought in that area at the time, which made it more likely that coyotes would have been in the area. It was pretty clear what had happened."

Swanson reported that coyotes had killed the cats by biting them in the head and neck, and then shaking them and tearing them apart. The organs had been devoured by the coyotes, who find them easier to digest than fur-covered flesh. "That was really unpleasant work," Swanson says. "But you do feel good about figuring out what happened."

The teenager who said he'd been killing cats admitted that he had been lying in an effort to impress other teens, and his mother got him professional help. Swanson was glad to have been able to establish that the teenager wasn't guilty of killing the cats.

"There's no question that this type of work is stressful and traumatic," Swanson says. "But it can be rewarding."

Perks

People who love animals take great satisfaction in being able to determine whether an animal has been wrongly killed, and to help find out why and how the crime was committed, and by whom. The job enables you to use problem-solving skills as well as previously acquired training and knowledge. Every case is different, which keeps the work interesting and challenging.

Get a Jump on the Job

Take all the biology and zoology courses that you can, and learn all that you can about animal anatomy. Get accustomed to working with animals, perhaps starting out in a pet store or as a helper to a local veterinarian. Observe the behavior of as many different animals as possible, particularly noting how they respond to other animals and to humans. Read everything you can find about animals, criminal cases involving animals, and the work of biologists, zoologists, animal pathologists, and animal forensic specialists.

ANIMAL SHELTER DIRECTOR

OVERVIEW

Working at an animal shelter isn't always an easy job, requiring you to come face to face with some very unpleasant situations involving animals. But at the same time, you're doing vital work that helps save the lives of lost, frightened, abandoned, or unwanted creatures. For every unpleasant situation you encounter, there are many more happy endings and wonderful stories of animals who find a warm, loving home.

Working in an animal shelter involves lots of different duties with a wide variety of animals. In addition to watching out for the basic needs of the animals, shelter caretakers must keep records of the animals received and discharged, along with any tests or treatments. Some shelter directors vaccinate newly admitted animals under the direction of a veterinarian or veterinary technician, and euthanize seriously ill, severely injured, or unwanted animals. Many shelters also offer surgery and spaying at reduced rates, along with educational outreach to local schools and community groups.

To be an animal shelter director means you've got to be good with animals and with people. You'll need to answer telephone inquiries, screen applicants for adoptions, and educate visitors about the importance of neutering and other animal health issues.

Working for private humane societies and animal shelters, it's inevitable that

AT A GLANCE

Salary Range

Average hourly wage for an animal shelter director is $8.21 an hour, with a range from $6.13 to $13.39.

Education/Experience

No set education is required, but experience with animals and animal training is desirable and expected. Most shelter directors have a certain amount of administrative work that needs to be done, and many directors are also experienced in dealing with people who have abused animals. Courses in animal control are offered at community colleges and some larger universities; classes are also offered through the National Animal Control Association.

Personal Attributes

It takes a special person to be able to work in an animal shelter, dealing with frightened, lost, sometimes-abused animals and members of the public who may be defensive, angry, or abusive. You need to be patient, sensitive, compassionate, and be able to keep a cool head and not show your anger when dealing with people who hurt or abuse animals.

Requirements

None.

Outlook

Demand for animal shelter directors is expected to remain steady as communities are increasingly recognizing the connection between animal abuse and abuse toward humans, according to the U.S. Department of Labor, and will probably continue to commit funds to animal shelters, many of which are working with social service agencies and law enforcement teams.

you'll need to deal with the public, some of whom might react with hostility to any implication that they are neglecting or abusing their pets. In these cases, you'll

Harry D. Brown III, animal shelter director

Harry Brown was a former steel worker who loved to hunt, and who started helping out at the Berks County (Pennsylvania) Animal Rescue League by trapping stray cats. "One day the director asked me if I'd be interested in doing their humane work," Brown recalls. "They wanted someone who could understand both sides of the fence—who'd understand that it was okay to have hunting dogs outside, and that hunting dogs need to be on the thin side." Eventually he was hired on full time as a certified animal control officer, and when the director announced her retirement, Brown stepped in to fill her shoes. He's been director for the past 16 years.

Brown loves the work. "I wished I would have done it years before," he says. Brown took courses and seminars in animal control through the University of Missouri in animal cruelty investigation and law enforcement, and by the time Pennsylvania passed a state law for directors requiring 56 hours in continuing education in small and large animals, he'd already taken more courses than he needed.

Brown says he likes the job because it's always different. "You never know from one day to the next, what's going down," he says. "You come in and think it's going to be a normal day, and then everything breaks loose." He explains he works a lot with the local drug task force, going along if there's a raid and animals are expected to be involved. He's also helped out when officers discovered a local cock-fighting ring.

Although Brown admits people often wonder how he can do the work he does, he explains that "as long as the good outnumbers the bad, it's a great job. You look at the animals you find homes for, the people write you back and tell you how it's working out, and it does make it worthwhile. We just adopted an eight-year-old terrier to an elderly lady, and if you could have seen the look on her face—well, it makes it all worthwhile."

Life at the Berks County Animal Rescue League is seldom peaceful or quiet. "At any given time, we have between 100 and 150 animals at the shelter. Right now, we also have two horses, a sheep, a goat, a llama, a peacock, and a duck."

Brown points out that the field has changed quite a bit from the old days, when no one really wanted to be the town dogcatcher. "It's becoming more and more of a professional, lifelong occupation," Brown says, attributing much of its newfound respectability to TV networks such as Animal Planet, which showcases *Animal Precinct,* a series that chronicles the drama, emotion, triumph, and tragedy of the work of the agents of the ASPCA Humane Law Enforcement Department, the only law enforcement group in New York City solely devoted to investigating crimes against New York's animal population.

Brown says he'd recommend a career in animal rescue to anyone. "More and more schools are making it mandatory to do some community service," he says. "Why not pick a local shelter and spend your community service there? If you enjoy working at the shelter, you'll enjoy it even more as an employee. If you're thinking about the animal rescue field, go to your local shelter and volunteer.

"Honestly, it's a great field, a very interesting and enjoyable career," Brown says. "The benefits are when you see a dog adopted out at eight weeks and then you see it come back at six months to be spayed and you see how it's grown. . . . It's wonderful to see the good home it has and how much joy it's brought."

need to maintain a calm and professional demeanor while you enforce the laws regarding animal care.

More and more training programs and workshops are available through the Humane Society of the United States, the American Humane Association, and the National Animal Control Association. Workshop topics include cruelty investigations, appropriate methods of euthanasia for shelter animals, proper guidelines for capturing animals, and techniques for preventing problems with wildlife. With experience and additional training, caretakers in animal shelters may become adoption coordinators, animal control officers, emergency rescue drivers, assistant shelter managers, or shelter directors.

Pitfalls

Starting salaries are significantly lower than those in many other fields, and some of the work may be unpleasant, physically and emotionally demanding, and sometimes dangerous. Animal shelter workers who witness abused animals or who must help euthanize unwanted, aged, or hopelessly injured animals may experience emotional stress. Most animal shelter directors may need to lift, hold, or restrain animals, risk-ing exposure to bites or scratches. Their work often involves kneeling, crawling, repeated bending, and lifting heavy supplies—not to mention being exposed to germicides or insecticides. The work setting can be noisy, and hours are irregular. In some animal shelters, someone must be on duty 24 hours a day, which means night shifts if a caretaker cannot make it to work.

Perks

If you love animals, and you want to help animals find better homes, working in an animal rescue organization can bring incredible satisfaction. Being part of the solution to animal problems is rewarding and can help you feel that your work really makes a difference.

Get a Jump on the Job

You can't be too young to start helping animals. Read a lot about them, learn to understand them, and see what your town is doing to help animals. You can volunteer in "breed rescue" kennels or your area's humane or animal rescue league even before you graduate from high school. This will give you a good idea about whether you'd like to do this kind of work for a living.

ANIMAL WRANGLER

OVERVIEW

Hollywood flamingos, pigs, and buffalo won't demand a limo filled with Perrier, or bowls of M&Ms with the red ones picked out—but animals on a Hollywood set do get special treatment. Whenever a film or TV show requires any sort of animal, someone's got to keep track of them on the shoot, training them and keeping them comfortable. That glamorous job belongs to the animal wrangler. If a director's script calls for a talking horse, a couple of cows that can lie down on command, a sheep wearing glasses, or a tap-dancing tarantula, it's the animal wrangler who gets the call.

Today, no one wrangler supplies all the animals for a shoot, because it's just too expensive. Typically, one wrangler outfit will get a general contract for a film, and that wrangler will contact others who specialize in specific animals. Most wranglers can work with a wide variety of animals in order to stay diversified for the ever-changing needs of the entertainment industry, but many specialize in just one breed. If a script calls for several palomino Arabian horses or a couple of black Clydesdales, a wrangler with the general contract (sometimes called the *animal coordinator*) will go out and find a wrangler specializing in horses to line up exactly what the director wants. Many wranglers say the hardest part of the job is being organized—not only do you have to be able to read and interpret new scripts and work out which animals may be needed, but you'll usually only have a couple of weeks to find any new ones you'll need.

AT A GLANCE

Salary Range

Experienced animal wranglers can earn as much as $650 a day. Annual salary can range from $25,000 to millions; the average is several hundred thousand dollars a year.

Education/Experience

In most states animal trainers are not required to have any specialized training in animal behavior, but many have been through a certification training program or have apprenticed to another professional animal trainer. College training in psychology or animal behavior is helpful. There are many private proprietary animal training schools as well as training programs offered by groups such as the Humane Society of the United States, the American Humane Association, the American Institute for Animal Science, the American Boarding Kennels Association, and the National Animal Control Association. Programs range from simple workshops on very specific animal training issues to a bachelor's of science degree in humane leadership for those who are interested in working in and running animal shelters. Schools offering programs in animal behavior include the Virginia-Maryland Regional College of Veterinary Medicine and the University of Maryland. Many animal trainers complete their training by doing an apprenticeship with a professional animal trainer after completing an animal training program.

Personal Attributes

All animal wranglers need sensitivity and experience with problem-solving and animal obedience. Certification is not mandatory, but several organizations offer training programs and certification for prospective animal trainers. It is also helpful to have excellent communication skills with both animals and humans. Wranglers must be incredibly patient, able to maintain their composure, and think clearly at all times, especially when working with large wild animals such as

(continues)

12

AT A GLANCE (continued)

tigers, lions, or elephants. Most wrangler jobs also require physical labor, since wranglers must clean cages or stables, and feed, groom, and transport their charges.

Requirements

Hollywood animal wranglers are often unionized, as are most employees in the film industry, although this is not an absolute requirement. Animal coordinators do not have to be unionized. Wranglers who are self-employed or who run a small business will often need to file "Doing Business As" (DBA) papers and tax forms, and acquire any other permits required under local and/or state ordinances. They may also be required to carry insurance and be bonded.

Outlook

Competition for jobs as an animal wrangler is very tight, and it can be difficult to break into the field.

The most important responsibility of an animal wrangler is to pretrain and condition his or her animals so they'll be able to perform any of the unusual things a film director might ask. In fact, wranglers spend most of their time training. Before shooting begins, a wrangler works with an animal so it isn't afraid once shooting starts, and so that the animal will be able to perform effectively. Animal wranglers train animals by accustoming the animal to human voice and contact, and conditioning the animal to respond to commands. You can use several techniques to train animals. Many trainers use a *bridge* technique, which involves a stimulus that a trainer uses to communicate the precise moment an animal does something right, offering positive reinforcement with food, toys, play, a rubdown, or the word *good*.

Animal training isn't typically something you can do quickly; instead, working on a sequence of small steps may take months or even years of repetition. During the conditioning process, trainers provide animals with mental stimulation and physical exercise, and often oversee other aspects of their care, such as diet preparation.

Once you're ready to take your animals to the set, your day begins by loading the animals and driving them (along with all the related paraphernalia, including food and water) to the filming location. On set, it's a waiting game as the tedious job of shooting a movie continues—some shoots last 14 hours or more. Your job focuses on getting the animals used to the environment. Wranglers always stick close by each individual animal on the set in order to keep them in position, safe, and secure. During shooting, the wrangler makes sure the animal stays out of the way until needed, and carefully waters, feeds, and grooms it until show time.

Once the shot with your animal is done, you'll probably need to hang around to see if any extra shots are needed. Then it's time to load up the animals, drive back home, and unload, clean, water, and feed the animals.

Animal wrangling is a highly specialized field that requires lots of training, continuing education, care, and compassion, but the rewards in job satisfaction and income can be significant.

Pitfalls

It may seem exciting and even a bit exotic, but animal wrangling is hard work with hours spent pretraining animals and even longer, often-tedious hours on the set. The pay scale for these jobs can be pretty low (unless you're union), since it's

Bobbi Colorado, animal wrangler

If you've watched *Secondhand Lions* or *Spy Kids,* you've seen the work of famed animal wrangler Bobbi Colorado, who's spent the past three decades working with creatures in film and television with husband and business partner Ken Beggs. She specializes in a wide range of animals, including her trained macaws and parrots and her gibbon Lolly (seen briefly in *Secondhand Lions* in the Arabic bazaar scene)—not to mention her border collie Seamus. One of Hollywood's top trainers, Colorado can coax animals to do just about anything; she can train a chicken to sit on a pig's head or get a dog to hit its mark on command without a lot of extra fuss.

Colorado grew up in the Bay Area of California, landing a job right after high school as a tour guide at Marine World in San Francisco. From there, she moved to Los Angeles where she met her future husband Ken, and worked with a wrangler who handled the animals for then-popular animal TV shows such as *Daktari* and *Gentle Ben*. "They must have been broke," she laughs, "because they hired me—and they didn't hire women back then. Now more than 50 percent of animal wranglers are women.

Eventually, she and her husband parlayed that experience into their own business, Bobbi Colorado and the Wild Bunch. "Actually, 'animal wrangler' is the name for animal people in the movie business," she says, "but I consider myself a trainer. Right now, I'm wrangling rats for a movie—I'm training them to go through a vent and come out on a roof en masse. That's kind of wrangling and training. Actually, wrangling is more like herding cattle. I train animals to do specific things for TV shows, movies, print media.

"As an animal coordinator, I coordinate getting the animals. But when a director tells me: 'We need to have three buffalo drinking out of a stream. . . . We need a cow to pretend it's tired and is lying down. . . . We need a rabbit running up to someone and sniffing their hands'—that's training."

For Colorado, it's all a labor of love. "For *Secondhand Lions*, we got four pigs from the slaughterhouse," she says. "They weighed 200 pounds apiece and they'd never been handled. Through food and love and affection, we taught them to walk on a lead, get into a truck, and to basically act like dogs. They had to be with a pack of dogs all the time. We trained them to sit, lie down, look right, look left, and follow an actor with the dog. To go from a 200-pound slaughterhouse pig and learn how to behave on set and do a good job—that's really something!" Colorado says it took her two months of prepping them to behave on the set. "Pigs are extremely smart," she says, "although they're not that affectionate. They're very food motivated, so it makes for a great animal to train."

This pig story has a happy ending: Once the movie was over, they became therapy pigs and are today helping autistic children. "They went from almost being on your plate to stardom to animal therapy!" Colorado laughs.

For her, the job is a dream come true, although it has its unpleasant moments. "My least favorite thing is being out on really cold or hot days, cleaning those cages," she says. "You still have to do all that. Probably the hardest thing for me to deal with is dealing with some difficult people

so competitive. Many wranglers will tell you that it can be a challenge to deal with some of the high-powered film people in Hollywood. Some directors and producers have little interest in animals and don't understand their special needs; othon a set. They say they want one thing, but when you get there you always have to be prepared for anything; it could be the total opposite." For instance, Colorado once trained 31 dogs for a TV commercial. "They wanted them to run up to a cage and bark," she says. "So I trained them, and when we got on set, they said: 'No, now we want them to walk slowly up to the cage and then sit.' You have some directors who have no consideration for animals. They think they don't need a rehearsal. They can give an actor 32 times to get a line right, but when an animal walks on set they think they should be able to perform perfectly right away. Most people have a lot of respect for the animals, but some people just don't. Fortunately, that doesn't happen very often."

When Colorado isn't on set wrangling her charges, she's working out of Dripping Springs' Sunrise Exotic Ranch, a nearby 325-acre spread owned by her friend Karen Glass. At the ranch, Colorado performs for school groups, church groups, scouts, with tours of the ranch and a bird show. "But then we teach the kids about the rainforest," she says. "When you get right down to it, it's really all about education." Exotic Ranch is home to 362 animals, including all the retired Ringling Brothers' chimpanzees, plus lemurs, monkeys, zebras and baby zebras, baby wildebeests, all types of hoof stock, ostriches, emus, and elk. In addition, the ranch boasts three bed-and-breakfast inns so people can come and stay the weekend and see the animals and learn about wildlife in general and how to save the earth. "We're such a throwaway society, but once the animals disappear, we're next," she says. "We're eating this earth like an apple, we're polluting the oceans. But I have high hopes. I'm really encouraged, I think people are headed in the right direction—trying anyway. I see a lot of young people who really care."

Although her movie work provides the money to feed the animals, her heart is really into educating kids about the animals as well as doing rescue work and providing a home for these animals who otherwise might have to be put down. "If you have passion and you love something enough, the money will follow," she says. "I worked for absolutely nothing to learn the trade."

Colorado recommends that aspiring animal wranglers do a lot of volunteer work with animal rescue, at shelters. "People like me are always looking for volunteers," she says. She also recommends Moorpark College in Southern California, which trains people to work with animals in a two-year program. "All of the big places hire graduates out of there, but you need to have a lot of volunteer experience to even be accepted there." Still, she notes that animal wrangling and training is hard work. "I see a lot of people who don't want to work very hard," she says. "I used to get volunteers and nothing was too hard. Now I say: 'Follow me around and see if you like this work.' But they just can't take it. It's pretty sad. They say: 'I'll do anything to work with animals' but two days later it's too hard. Being a trainer or a wrangler is not just playing with animals."

At the end of the day, she simply enjoys being with her animals. "The thing I like best about my job is being alone with my animals with nobody else around, and just enjoying watching them playing with each other. I'm very lucky to have found a career that I love and am passionate about as well as make money at."

ers frequently change their demands at a moment's notice. Some of the work may be unpleasant, smelly, physically and emo-tionally demanding, and dangerous. Animals can bite and refuse to do what you ask. Furthermore, animal wranglers often work outdoors in all kinds of weather, and hours are often long and irregular.

Perks

If you love animals and you're good with them, and you enjoy the idea of working in the movies for famous directors and meeting movie stars, this could be the perfect job for you. You'll get lots of Hollywood exposure, and the perks—trips, salary, free food, and so on—are terrific. In this field, just about every job is different and you'll never know what that next phone call will bring.

Get a Jump on the Job

You can start by reading a lot about animals and learning how to understand them. Volunteer at a breed rescue kennel, stable, farm, zoo, or your area's humane or animal rescue league. See if you can get any sort of part-time work with a trainer or breeder of the particular animal you're interested in working with. This will give you a good idea about what it's like to work with this type of animal.

AQUARIST

OVERVIEW

If you've been tending to multiple aquariums in your home since you were six, you could be headed for a career as an aquarist. An aquarist is the person you'll find working at an aquarium exhibit, feeding the fish, checking to make sure all the creatures are healthy, treating sick fish and animals, and keeping a close watch on behavior. Some of the work is fascinating and high profile, but other aspects—such as scrubbing down the aquariums—can be messy, smelly, and pretty tedious. It's all in a day's work for an aquarist.

Aquarium exhibits are costly, so there's lots of pressure on staff to make sure the fish remain healthy and happy. Every living creature coming into the aquarium must first be quarantined and carefully observed to make sure that they're healthy and won't spread any diseases to the rest of the exhibit population.

Although most aquarists spend most of their time at the aquarium exhibit, some are responsible for acquiring new fish and animals for the exhibits. This involves working in a location other than an aquarium setting. In fact, some aquarists spend most of their time in the ocean, looking for and gathering fish to be exhibited at an aquarium.

It takes a lot of work to maintain a successful and healthy aquarium exhibit, and an aquarist is expected to oversee all that's involved in doing so. You'll need to maintain cleaning tools and supplies, do constant checks to make sure the water quality is up to snuff, and make sure that routine care occurs on schedule. Filter systems also must be carefully maintained to assure water quality.

In addition, aquarists conduct research. They might investigate the best method of feeding or caring for a particular species of fish, or observe how fish interact with one another, how they mate, and what their habits are. It's important to have a good understanding of marine life and habitat, and to understand the relationship between different species of marine life and their environments.

Wayne Stempler, aquarist

Wayne Stempler grew up fascinated by all forms of aquatic life, and after earning a bachelor's degree in environmental science, he started learning on the job. Today, an aquarist for 25 years, he's the senior keeper and aquarist at the New York Aquarium in Brooklyn.

"I've always enjoyed everything about aquatic life," Stempler says. "There wasn't much question in my mind that I'd end up working with it."

As senior keeper and aquarist at the New York Aquarium, with more than 8,000 animals, he's responsible for a section of tanks, including the aquarium's quarantine area.

"When fish first come in, they need to be quarantined to make sure they don't have any diseases," Stempler explains. "I work hand in hand with the pathology laboratory in that capacity." It's particularly rewarding, he says, to see new fish become acclimated. "It's always exciting when you see them start to eat and to thrive in their new surroundings."

The biggest challenge in his job, he notes, is caring for the live coral. It's difficult to get the coral to grow and reproduce, he says, and it can be disappointing if the coral does not grow as well as expected.

As part of his job, he also keeps an eye on the filter systems of his tanks, feeds and checks on the fish, removes fish that have died, and performs many other tasks. Stempler enjoys the variety of work his job entails, and says he's never bored and no two days are the same. "No day here is typical, because you're dealing with live animals," he says.

Pitfalls

Aquariums aren't found in every town in America, so jobs for aquarists tend to be somewhat limited. The jobs that are available tend to be competitive, so you may need to consider education extending beyond a bachelor's degree. Because the job is physically demanding, it may become difficult to perform all required duties as you become older.

Perks

The job is varied, and most aquarists find it to be very rewarding because they get to work closely with aquatic life and assure that they have clean and healthy surroundings and are well cared for. Working at an aquarium offers a great way to further your academic interests through research. If you love aquatic life, you'll enjoy learning more and more about a fascinating topic. Because the job involves so many different aspects, the boredom factor is extremely low.

Get a Jump on the Job

Aquarists say the only way to really get to know what the job is like is to complete an internship at an aquarium. Only then, they say, can you decide whether or not the work is for you. If you're lucky enough to live close to an aquarium, ask if there are any volunteer opportunities available. Meanwhile, visit an aquarium and pay close attention to what the staff is doing. Check out aquarium Web sites to see if you can contact employees for some personal career advice. And read everything you can about marine biology and aquariums.

ASSISTANCE DOG TRAINER

OVERVIEW

Although many people think of assistance dogs as primarily animals who help blind people, assistance dog trainers actually work with four types of assistance dogs: Seeing Eye dogs, hearing dogs, seizure alert dogs, and disability assistance dogs. Trainers are responsible for teaching these animals very specific skills that enable them to serve their owners.

Seeing Eye dogs help blind and visually impaired people avoid obstacles, stop at curbs and steps, and negotiate traffic. These dogs wear a harness and U-shaped handle to help the dog and the handler communicate. The human provides directional commands and the dog ensures the handler's safety—even if this means disobeying an unsafe command.

Hearing dogs are trained to serve deaf or hard-of-hearing people, alerting to the sound of a doorbell, a knock on the door, a fire alarm, an oven buzzer, a telephone ring, a baby cry, a name call, or a smoke alarm. When a sound occurs, these dogs are trained to make physical contact with the owner and lead the deaf person to the source of the sound.

Seizure alert dogs are trained to recognize the onset of a seizure in its owner. Often, the animal can sense an oncoming seizure before the owner can, and can alert the person that it's coming. The dog also is trained to summon help if a seizure has begun.

Disability assistance dogs are trained to help owners with mental or emotional disabilities remain calm and functioning,

AT A GLANCE

Salary Range
An assistance dog trainer can expect to earn between $18,000 and $33,000 a year (or an average of about $10 an hour), depending on location, the employer, and other factors.

Education/Experience
While there are no firm educational requirements, most agencies prefer assistance dog trainers to have a college degree. A degree in a field such as animal management, which includes courses in animal science and psychology, would be valuable.

Personal Attributes
You must have the ability to teach both animals and people, as it's likely that you'll not only be training dogs, but teaching people how to get along with their dogs, as well. You should be able to empathize with the people to whom you will be providing dogs, but not be pitying or condescending. You should relate well to all types of people, have excellent communication skills, and be willing to do a variety of tasks, many of which are not glamorous, such as the cleaning of stalls and cages. Training dogs is physically demanding, so you'll need to be in very good shape.

Requirements
Requirements will vary, depending on the employer and the circumstances of employment, but typically include experience in training dogs and the willingness to work outdoors in all types of weather.

Outlook
These jobs are expected to increase about as fast as average through 2012, according to government predictions.

and help owners with physical disabilities perform daily tasks, such as picking up dropped items, pulling wheelchairs, opening and closing doors, turning lights off and on, and helping the owner walk by providing balance. Service dogs wear a backpack or harness.

The ideal assistance dog loves people and isn't protective, is not too active, and is confident but not dominant or submissive. Most assistance dogs are either golden retrievers or Labrador retrievers. Dogs such as German shepherds are easy to train, but they tend to be too protective, and field dogs such as English setters are often more interested in their environment than people. Small dogs can't pick up large objects or pull wheelchairs, and large dogs don't fit very well under a table in a restaurant or out of the way on a plane. Hearing dogs are often friendly mixed breed rescues in all different sizes and shapes, although most are small to medium-sized dogs, and energetic enough so that they're ready to work as soon as they hear a target sound.

Although there are basic obedience rules, every assistance dog is different, and there are many aspects to the training that require individual care and consideration. Dog trainers must be very patient, because it generally takes six to nine months to prepare a dog for service. The dogs will need to be trained in a number of areas to be a successful assistance dog; first comes basic behaviors, which will build on what will later become trained tasks. Next comes training for specific tasks (a Seeing Eye vs. a hearing dog, for example), one of the final stages of training. A candidate dog must first be socialized with people, animals, and a wide variety of environments so that it can learn to behave calmly in public. The dog must be trained to pay exclusive attention to its handler in the face of all sorts of distractions, and learn verbal and hand signal cues for safety, obedience, and assistance work. Some dogs are trained to work with certain kinds of equipment,

such as a special harness that can be used to help the owner maintain balance. In addition, the assistance dog must learn how to train and work as a team.

The day starts early for an assistance dog trainer, with feeding and watering, setting up training areas, exercising the animals, and training. Most trainers use praise, positive reinforcement, and clickers to train their animals, which is an ongoing process for assistance dogs.

Dogs are pack animals, and they obey whoever they understand to be the leader of the pack. As a dog trainer, you have to convince a dog that you're the pack leader, and the animal must obey you. You'll need to know how to interact properly with each animal.

Trainers normally work with several dogs at a time—often as many as eight or more at once. Assistance dog trainers work 35 hours a week, Monday to Friday, with occasional evenings, weekends, and holidays. Most experts figure that it takes about one or two hours of daily training over six months to train an assistance dog.

In addition, the trainer works with clients, matching them with a dog that fits the person's temperament and teaching the person how to use the dog in the most effective manner. Trainers can produce about 500 to 600 assistance dogs each year, and the average waiting list to obtain a dog is two years.

Most assistance dog trainers start out as an apprentice with an assistance program for two to three years.

Pitfalls

There aren't a lot of people who train assistance dogs. In fact, there are fewer than 30,000 people in the whole country who earn a living doing this work. If you get hired as an assistance dog trainer, you shouldn't expect to make a lot of money. The agencies

Kathy Zubrycki and Amy McPherson, assistance dog trainers

Kathy Zubrycki trains guide dogs for Guiding Eyes, a New York–based organization that trains guide dogs and matches them with visually impaired and blind clients. Amy McPherson is employed by Canine Companions for Independence, a California-based organization that trains dogs and matches them with people who are visually impaired or hard-of-hearing, blind, deaf, physically handicapped, or who suffer from emotional disorders.

"The rewards are tremendous," McPherson says. "To be able to facilitate the relationship between these specially trained dogs and their human partners is something very few people can say that they do."

McPherson works primarily with dogs that are being trained to assist deaf people, while Zubrycki trains guide dogs to help blind individuals. Zubrycki explains that dogs that will be successful as guide dogs must have confidence, be friendly, be focused and not easily distracted, be able to accept changes in their environment, and have a willingness to please.

Dogs with those characteristics, she says, are not difficult to train and make wonderful companions. Formal training for guide dogs begins at Guiding Eyes when a puppy is 16 to 18 months old. The dog, however, will have been raised by a volunteer who has exposed it to general training and a variety of environments. That helps the dog to be prepared for the more specific training necessary for it to become a successful guide dog.

At Canine Companions for Independence, puppies begin training at 8 weeks. It normally takes between six and nine months of advanced training to prepare a dog to serve as an assistance animal, McPherson says, but hearing dogs can sometimes be trained in as little as four months.

For McPherson, the biggest challenge she faces in her job is communicating with the people who are being paired with the hearing dogs. Deaf people use a variety of techniques to communicate, including American Sign Language (ASL), reading lips, and writing notes. Because ASL uses a different sentence structure than English, it can be difficult to communicate in writing, and one-on-one contact is no easier. "Without an interpreter present during face-to-face interactions, I am severely limited in my communication abilities," McPherson says.

For Zubrycki, the most difficult part of the job is understanding how each dog perceives his or her environment, and how the dog accepts the training. "In order for any training to be successful, the trainer must first develop a relationship with and an understanding of the dog," Zubrycki says. "All dogs, like people, are different and require different handling techniques to facilitate the learning process."

Both women agree that the key to working as an assistance dog trainer is to get as much experience as possible working with dogs and other animals. "It's very physical work and can [be] difficult at times," Zubrycki warns. "Someone coming into this career must be a self starter, have a lot of initiative, and be willing to work long hours."

Getting some experience working with dogs will help you decide if you're cut out for the job, McPherson adds. "Experience working with dogs will tell you if you have the patience necessary to work in this field," she says. "You'll learn if you'll be comfortable around barking dogs, dogs that are stressed, and if you're okay with getting dirty and covered with dog hair every day. Actually working with dogs will let you know whether you're prepared for the physical aspects of the job, and if you'll be comfortable working your way up from a very entry-level position."

that run dog-training programs are generally nonprofit organizations that depend on donations and grants to make ends meet. As a result, salaries are low considering the amount of time and work that's expected.

Moreover, training dogs can be frustrating work, because some dogs just aren't suited to the type of training necessary for service dogs. And yet, despite the hard work and low salary, the field is competitive, because lots of people want to train assistance dogs.

This is a very active job with a lot of walking and outdoor work in all types of weather; there is often a lot of travel as you visit dogs and their owners. Some trainers get overly attached to the animals and have a hard time giving up the dogs to the people they've been trained to serve.

Perks

Assistance dog trainers love their work and find it to be extremely rewarding. If you love dogs, and you enjoy helping people, this is the perfect combination of both. You'll get the personal satisfaction over and over of knowing that you've made someone's life better through your work.

Get a Jump on the Job

Get as much experience working with and training dogs as you can. Volunteer at your local pet shelter or Humane Society, offer to help train your neighbors' puppies, and read all that you can about the training of dogs. Contact a dog trainer in your area and ask if you can observe some training sessions. If there's an assistance dog training center in your area, inquire about volunteer opportunities. Perhaps you, with the help of your family, could raise a puppy that will later be trained as an assistance dog. For example, Guide Dogs for the Blind currently has more than 1,000 volunteer puppy raisers (beginning at age 9 and up) in the western states alone. You receive a pup of about eight weeks of age, and you're responsible for housetraining, teaching basic obedience and good manners, and—above all—socializing them to the world. As a guide dog puppy raiser, no prior experience is necessary; you'll become a part of a guide dog puppy-raising club, receive instructional materials, and have local expert guidance. (See Appendix A for more information.)

DOG DAY CARE OWNER

OVERVIEW

Thirty or forty years ago, when most dads went out to work and moms stayed home, there was always someone around to take the family pooch out for a romp or a potty break. But today, time is a priceless commodity—and most families include two working parents who don't have the time to care for a dog. With the whole family at work and at school, the family dog is the only one left at home to mope and become depressed. The modern solution—leaving the family dog at a special "day care" facility—can provide the experienced dog handler with a terrific career. You'll find dog day care centers like these popping up all over the country. It makes sense to many families not just to ease separation anxiety while owners work, but also as a good place to take the dog while the carpets are being cleaned or the house fumigated for insects, if the family is having a party or remodeling a home, or even if you just need to be out of the house for a few hours while it's being shown by a realtor to a prospective buyer.

Dog day care is different from a more traditional kennel in several ways. First, in day care the dogs are only brought in during the day while their owners are at work. (Some owners bring their dogs to a day care center simply to help socialize the animal.) Also, kennels traditionally separate pets and forbid them to play together; many kennels will not even allow two dogs from the same household to stay together.

AT A GLANCE

Salary Range

Dog owners pay anywhere from $15 to $40 a day for day care services, depending on location, and whether a dog drops in for the day or its owner has a longer-term contract. Income for dog day care owners varies depending on location and size of business, but typically may range from about $36,400 to $70,000 a year.

Education/Experience

Experience with problem-solving and animal obedience is helpful. Several organizations offer training programs and certification in animal training, including the Humane Society of the United States, the American Humane Association, the American Institute for Animal Science, the American Boarding Kennels Association, and the National Animal Control Association. Experience in business and marketing is also extremely helpful.

Personal Attributes

You'll need to love dogs, be patient and sensitive, and have excellent communication skills.

Requirements

Dog training and handling experience is very important; loving dogs doesn't mean you'll automatically know how to handle various dog problems. You should also be expert in canine first aid, CPR, and animal behavior. Many locations have local and state regulations and requirements, so you may need registration and licenses. In addition, a dog day care owner who is self-employed or who runs a small business will often need to file "Doing Business As" (DBA) papers and tax forms, and acquire any other permits required under local and/or state ordinances. You also may be required to carry insurance and be bonded. The center will need to have an enclosed yard in addition to indoor space; kennel cages are also a necessity.

(continues)

Doggie day care, however, encourages dogs—which are pack animals and thrive on togetherness—to romp together in a "common room." This is why day care costs may be slightly higher than boarding—because the ratio of staff to dogs is high so that the dogs may be constantly supervised.

The basic idea behind dog day care is simple—you provide a safe and healthy atmosphere with lots of human and dog interaction. Dogs can play with other dogs, lie around chewing on a favorite toy, play with humans, nap on a dog bed, or run around outside and play. The most important aspect of dog day care is that the dog isn't languishing at home alone.

Proponents say the benefits are significant. Pets develop interpersonal skills with other animals and separation anxiety virtually disappears. Day cares that offer lots of exercise can actually improve a dog's physical condition, and the dog returns home happier than when he left.

Dog day care centers sometimes offer other services, including overnight boarding, training, spa services, and grooming, as well as extras such as birthday parties, canine massage and aromatherapy treatments, or checkups by visiting vets. Some centers sell dog treats, toys, sweaters, collars, and leashes.

Typically, on the first day for a new dog, the owner of the center meets each new customer and puts the dog through a screening test to be sure that aggression, shyness, or fear won't be a problem. A typical test would involve pulling on the dog's ears and its collar, judging its reaction to noise, and checking for food aggression. Most screening processes include interviews with the client followed by evaluation of the dog in various circumstances. Next, the owner introduces a new dog one-on-one with other dogs to see how they interact, and then puts the new dog into a small group of four or five compatible dogs. Most day care establishments require that dogs have annual vaccinations for distemper, hepatitis, parvo virus, and Bordatella (kennel cough), with up-to-date rabies inoculations and preventives for fleas, ticks, and heartworms. Dogs must be spayed or neutered.

The centers are usually established in large, open spaces that can be divided to provide separate areas for napping and play. Most have an outdoor exercise area as well as large indoor space and a time-out area for dogs that get too excited or aggressive. Some centers provide special beds or dog furniture and many have tunnels and play equipment. All have toys for play.

Dan Highley, dog day care owner

If you're a dog in central Texas, there's probably no place you'd rather be than relaxing at the High-Stone Pet Lodge run by Dan and Della Highley.

Dan Highley and a business partner own the Dallas day care center, and wife Della manages it. "She's the one who makes it go," Dan Highley explains. Della has more than 30 years of experience in the pet industry, including working with breeders, vets, and kennel/grooming operations in three different states and abroad, where she established a grooming/boarding business in Athens, Greece, for five years. In addition, Della and Dan breed and show Lakeland terriers across the United States and Canada, and understand how to promote healthy, happy, well-groomed pets.

Attorney Dan brings an extensive background in management and small business operations from his 30-plus years in commercial real estate and law.

For the past six years, Dan and Della have pooled their expertise at High-Stone. Dan Highley attributes the success of their business partly to the fact that they can offer grooming and boarding in addition to day care.

"You need all three to make ends meet," he says. High-Stone's day care is a good option if owners want to keep their dog entertained while they're at work, or if the family wants to remove a dog from the stress of a crowded house during family gatherings or other special occasions. But in addition to its high-quality doggie day care, High-Stone also offers dogs individual beds, private quarters, and the option of overnight lodging with optional luxury suites and salon grooming.

High-Stone's day care program includes a day-long structured program alternating different types of music with exercise and play in air-conditioned, climate-controlled comfort. The day care offers treadmill time, ball playing, and lots of love and personal attention, and is one of the few establishments nationwide to affiliate with Yuppy Puppy Dog Care Canada, Inc., where doggie day care began.

Although High-Stone has more than 12 outdoor runs, the dogs usually play indoors. Treats include ice in their bowls and Frosty Paws (doggie ice cream) on hot days. All dogs spend four hours in the playroom—large dogs in the morning and smaller dogs in the afternoon. On average, about 25 or 30 large dogs are playing together at one time. Costs for day care are $16 a day (or a weekly pass for $70), with overnight stays ranging from $18 to $35 a night.

In the overnight kennel, each dog has an individual bed in private quarters; for an additional fee, owners can book their dog into a luxury "bed and breakfast" eight-foot suite. These special rooms include an individual Disney TV with "Mickey Mouse Ear" speakers playing animal animated movies throughout the day, relaxing background music at night, a comfy bed and mattress, and a special retro bowl with a custom mat. Instead of a wire door, each suite has a glass front door that opens to the daily activity in the day care area, plus a window. Outdoor exercise for luxury suite guests is scheduled three times a day, and additional dogs may share a suite for the night.

Showcased in the *Dallas Morning News* and on the American Kennel Club Web site, High-Stone also offers grooming and salon services supervised by a master certified groomer with more than 30 years of grooming experience in the United States and Europe.

(continues)

(continued)

If running a dog day care center sounds like fun to you, Highley emphasizes that you need both lots of experience with dogs and with business. "You should have some experience in the animal industry," he says. "It's best if you've been in dog shows, and that you understand the breeds, genetic predispositions to diseases, and temperaments. If you have that background, then you need to team up with someone with a business background so you can comply with state and federal rules and regulations on payroll, income tax returns, income, and expenses. It's not just a fun thing to go into just because you like animals.

"An MBA is really helpful," he says. "Spend some time working in the business first. Find out whether this is really something where you want to devote your time. Make sure you prepare a good business plan and figure it all out. Most people I see get into it because they think dogs are fun. But a few of the bigger ones know that it's all about cash flow management and the business end of things.

"You don't sit around and play with dogs all day, which is what people think you do," Highley says. Instead, the day care's 11 employees spend their time taking care of the pets, grooming, exercising, checking pets in and out, and working on administrative issues.

One of the best things about the business is that you'll meet a lot of people and you'll develop great relationships—almost like an extended family, Highley says—with a lot of customers.

The stress of making the business financially stable is significant, he believes, and the liability issues are always present. "There is a liability side to the animal-related business," he says, "if there is any injury to an animal. If a dog dies while in your custody, even if it was because of a pre-existing medical problem, you could have a problem." It helps, he says, that both he and his partner are attorneys, and the fact that they are also experts in real estate helped them when it came to establishing the business and complying with zoning laws. "Those are tough issues for an animal-related business, because there is a lot of barking that can relate to nuisance claims."

The busiest days are right after the holidays, he says. "The day after Thanksgiving, we had 90 dogs to be groomed and more than 100 dogs were going home, so we had 100 transactions to be processed. The day after Thanksgiving, Christmas, spring break, the Fourth of July—those days we just get slammed."

Dogs are extremely social creatures that enjoy being part of a pack. Many develop problems when left alone for hours at a time. In fact, many dogs experience separation anxiety when left alone during the day, destroying furniture or clothes, having accidents in the house, and barking constantly. Dog day care can be a tremendous help to these dogs and their owners. Interacting and playing together at dog day care is an ideal environment for a dog's instinctual "pack" behavior. At dog day care, puppies and dogs learn valuable communication and social skills by interacting with other dogs of all ages.

Dog owners love the idea, because their dogs come home calm and ready for sleep—and because they are around other dogs and people, they become much more comfortable with visitors. Owners feel better knowing their pets will get exercise and socialization—and they won't have to come home to chewed-up shoes and sofa cushions as a result of separation anxiety. The owner can go off to work and not feel so guilty. At the end of the day, many day care services provide the owners with a written report about their dog's day. Some larger centers have installed Web cameras so their owners can watch the dogs at work via computer.

While most dogs thrive in day care, geriatric dogs typically don't adjust quite so well and don't really enjoy the boisterousness of day care, and some breeds—such as the more aggressive chows—just don't do well.

Almost anyone can start a dog day care center, although owning and running a dog day care business requires a bigger financial investment than a pet-sitting or dog walking business, because the day care center requires a fairly large physical space that is typically regulated by each state and locality. In fact, getting a site and permits is often more complicated than most people expect because of local ordinances regarding animals.

You can start a business for less than $20,000 if you already have the space and the permits, but if you've got to rent or buy a place, the cost will be higher—at least $50,000. Alternatively, you can buy a dog day care franchise, which streamlines the process of opening a business by offering equipment, training, computer software, signs, and marketing. For example, D.O.G. Development was the first in the nation to franchise dog day care and boarding facilities. Today, the company has sold 33 Camp Bow Wow franchises.

If space allows and you've got tolerant neighbors, you can open a day care at your home, but a better alternative is to rent commercial warehouse space and convert it into a dog day care spa, complete with water features, fenced outdoor space, and indoor couches to ensure your clients have all the creature comforts they're used to at home. Some innovative day care centers installed Web cams so owners at work can log onto the day care Web site and see live footage of their dogs playing with other dogs

Pitfalls

Most people love animals, and running a dog day care center may seem like a walk in the park—but remember that taking care of a bunch of dogs, all with different personalities and requirements, can be hard work. You'll need to train, feed, water, groom, bathe, and exercise the animals, and clean, disinfect, and repair their cages. You'll also need to play with the dogs, provide companionship, and watch out for any behavioral changes that could indicate illness or injury. Dog day care is also a business, with all of the headaches a business entails—including liability.

Perks

Once you open your doors you'll be surprised at how many people are out there who don't want to keep their pets alone for long periods of time during the day. This can be a lucrative career if you love dogs and are willing to invest the time and energy it takes to be successful.

Get a Jump on the Job

If you love dogs and you think you'd like to run a doggie day care business, start by getting lots of experience with dogs. Try walking dogs for your neighbors, or starting a neighborhood pet-sitting service. Volunteer at a kennel, a vet's office, a pet store, a breed rescue group, or an animal shelter. This will give you lots of hands-on experience in taking care of dogs and understanding how different the breeds can be. You also can read as much as possible about training and kennels.

DOG GROOMER

OVERVIEW

Whether it's a cut, curl, shampoo, or nail painting, dog groomers specialize in making pooches beautiful. Some groomers operate their own businesses, while others work in kennels, animal shelters, pet-supply stores, and in veterinary offices. Still other groomers maintain mobile grooming facilities—kind of like a dog spa on wheels—and travel to their clients, which can be a boon to dogs who get nervous when they have to go to the groomer.

Dog groomers wash and cut canine coats, and maintain dogs' appearance and health by clipping claws, cleaning teeth and ears, and treating parasites. The basic grooming of a dog involves several steps: The initial brushing is followed by clipping with electric clippers, combs, and grooming shears; the groomer then cuts the nails, cleans the ears, bathes, and blow-dries the animal, and ends with a final clipping and styling.

Although there are standards detailing the look of different dog breeds, pet owners may have their own idea of how Fido should be clipped and styled. It's the job of the groomer to satisfy the customer, even if he or she thinks the dog would look better with a different style. If the pet owner isn't happy with your work, chances are you won't see him or her again.

If you're interested in being a dog groomer, you'll often need to do more than just pop a pup into the bath and do some light clipping. Groomers often become advisors to pet owners, offering information about dog diets, caring for the animal's

AT A GLANCE

Salary Range

Salaries of dog groomers vary greatly, depending on clientele, location, the amount of work, and employer. A pet groomer who works for a large pet-retail company can expect to earn about $7.50 per hour, plus half of the fees charged. Private groomers set their own rates, normally charging between $30 and $50 to bathe, dry, cut, and style a dog. Groomers often receive tips from customers, as well. Annual salaries may range from $40,000 to $60,000 a year.

Education/Experience

There are no educational requirements for dog grooming, but there are dog grooming schools where you can learn the preferred cuts for different breeds and other aspects of grooming. Knowledge of dog breeds and their characteristics is very important, as well. Animal education courses would be helpful.

Personal Attributes

You should have an affection and respect for animals. You'll need to be able to stand for significant periods of time, and must be in fairly good physical condition to be able to handle the dogs you groom. It helps to have a calm personality and lots of patience, since dogs aren't always cooperative. Excellent communication and public relations skills are vital.

Requirements

Most states do not require a license to operate a dog grooming business, but voluntary certification is available from a number of organizations. In addition, a groomer who is self-employed or who runs a small business will often need to file "Doing Business As" (DBA) papers and tax forms, and acquire any other permits required under local and/or state ordinances. Groomers also may be required to carry insurance and be bonded.

(continues)

AT A GLANCE (continued)

Outlook

Good. Dog grooming has been a steadily growing industry, and is expected to continue to grow as people continue to spend more money on pets. The number of jobs for groomers is expected to increase more quickly than average through 2012—pet groomers should grow by 12 percent, according to government statistics. The $32 billion pet care industry is expanding at nearly 5 percent annually, and since 43 percent of U.S. households have at least one dog, there is room for all sizes and types of dog-related businesses such as grooming services. Pet owners tend to spend more on animal services when the economy is strong. The dog population is expected to increase, and pet owners (including a large number of baby boomers, whose disposable income is expected to increase as they age) will need to take advantage of grooming services. As many pet owners increasingly consider their pet as part of the family, their demand for luxury animal services and willingness to spend greater amounts of money on their pet will continue to grow. However, job opportunities in grooming may vary from year to year, because the strength of the economy affects demand in this field.

---

coat, and other canine matters. Because a groomer gets a close look at the dog during the grooming process, and because these experts see hundreds of dogs, the groomer is often the one who spots a medical condition such as a sore or an ear infection, before it becomes too serious. Most groomers offer flea and tick treatments for dogs.

As more pet products and services become available, pet owners have exhibited a willingness to spend big bucks on their dogs. As a result, some groomers are branching out to offer moisturizing treatments, exotic styling, massage, and special skin care services.

To be a dog groomer, you'll need to learn how to clip, scissor, bathe, and blow-dry, as well as understand dog behavior and proper handling. There are two main ways to train as a dog groomer: You can serve as an apprentice, learning on the job with an experienced, qualified groomer, or you can attend a private dog grooming school. Both of these methods will help you gain practical experience under supervision. There are 50 state-licensed grooming schools throughout the country, with programs varying in length from two to 18 weeks. The National Dog Groomers Association of America certifies groomers who pass a written examination consisting of 400 questions (including some on cats), with a separate part testing practical skills. Beginning groomers often start by taking on one job at a salon, such as bathing and drying a dog, eventually assuming responsibility for the entire grooming process from the initial brush-out to the final clipping. Groomers who work in large establishments or kennels may eventually move into supervisory or managerial positions.

Experienced groomers often choose to open their own shops. When you're ready to branch out into your own business, you'll need to make sure you have the right organizational and business skills as well as the ability to work well with pets, and you'll need to get the word out about your business. If you treat your customers well and do a good job with their pets, customers will tell their friends about you. Word-of-mouth advertising is very effective, and it's a great way to build up a clientele. You also might consider posting signs about your services in public places, getting yourself listed in the business section of the phone book, or running an ad in your local paper.

Debra Goodman, dog groomer

Debra Goodman was trained to groom dogs at the New York School of Dog Grooming in New York City. But the best training, she says, comes from years of practice.

Goodman was lucky, she says, because a skilled groomer at her very first place of employment took her under his wing and trained her. That, coupled with the school experience and a lot of practice, have made her proficient as a groomer. Her dog grooming salon in the basement of her Pennsylvania home boasts a separate entrance, which keeps the dogs she grooms apart from her own pets and family.

She limits her practice to a manageable number of dogs because she likes to take her time with each animal, most of which she has come to know. She enjoys working with all breeds, and while Goodman says she loves all dogs, she admits that not all dogs love her. "That was hard for me to accept for a while, but I finally got used to the fact that not every dog was going to be crazy about me," she says. "Some dogs are cranky to be here, and they'd rather be anyplace else."

While she enjoys working on her own and being able to work from home, Goodman says there are some downsides to the business. Clients sometimes cancel at the last minute, giving her less work than she'd counted on. She must pay a yearly license fee to operate the business from her home, and, like other self-employed people, she faces issues with insurance and other business-related matters. Although she very much enjoys working with dogs and can't think of any job she'd rather do, she warns that grooming dogs is work—not play. "There's a lot of hair flying around, and you have to stand up all day," she says. "I'd recommend that somebody observe dog grooming for a while before you decide for sure it's what you want to do."

And there's always the possibility that a dog will take exception to whatever you're doing and bite you. "I've never been bitten badly enough to need to go to the hospital, but it has happened [to some other groomers]," she says. "The longer you work with dogs, the better you're able to read them, and most of the time a bite can be avoided. But it happens. I guess it's just a hazard of the trade."

It's important that you learn about any licensing or zoning requirements that might affect your business. You'll also need to have the skills and organization to schedule appointments; pay and manage employees, if applicable; keep track of billing and payment records; and determine what taxes you owe.

Pitfalls

Even the most experienced dog groomer sometimes ends up with a dog that won't cooperate, or a pet owner who doesn't like your work. Dealing with customers can be challenging, and groomers occasionally get bitten by unhappy animals. You'll be standing for significant periods of time, which can be tiring. And, it's a sure bet that you'll be covered with dog hair for a good portion of your workday. If you start your own business, you'll need to buy special tools, including scissors, electric clippers, toenail clippers, and hairdryers. Some groomers will clean a dog's teeth, which requires special equipment. And if you're faced with a tough job, you can't take your work home with you or leave it for the next day—you've got to finish every dog you've got that day, even if it means you have to stay late.

Perks

People who go into dog grooming as a career generally love being around animals and enjoy their work. If you have the proper location and space available in your home, you may be able to start a home-based business. If you work for yourself, you can enjoy a flexible schedule.

Get a Jump on the Job

Start learning about styles for different breeds of dogs by reading and researching on the Internet. Ask a dog groomer if you can watch him or her work. After you have an idea of how the work is done, practice on your own dog. Get as much experience working with dogs as you can. Talk to lots of different established dog groomers to try to figure out if this is the right career for you. Ask to spend a full day observing the operation of a busy pet salon, paying close attention to the physical requirements you'll need to handle the day-to-day business of grooming.

DOG HANDLER

OVERVIEW

The spotlight comes up, the fans in the stands are hushed, and out into the ring runs a gorgeous dog on a leash, led by a neatly dressed professional. At a signal from the judge, the handler runs down the center of the ring with the dog trotting happily alongside, tail erect and eyes bright. Later, tempted by bits of food or treats, the show dog stands perfectly still as the judge's hands move over its body.

If it looks easy, that's only because the handler has practiced this exercise countless times. When you're watching the work of a professional dog show handler—someone who is trained to show a purebred dog to best advantage—it all seems completely simple. But the easier it looks, the more likely the handler has worked hard to make it look that way.

There are three parts of a conformation dog show, in which purebred dogs are evaluated to determine how well they represent the breed standard. The three parts include the breed competition, the group competition, and the best in show competition. The first part of the competition is among the dogs in each class within the breed. Dogs in each of the classes are judged with the best dog in each class moving ahead in competition. After all of the classes have been judged, the best of male and best of female classes are judged. The winner of those classes then competes for the best of winners prize. These two dogs are awarded points by the end of the breed competition, depending on the number of dogs they've beaten within the breed. These points go towards their own cham-

pionship title. The final stage in the breed competition brings in "specials," a new class of dogs that were not yet judged during this show. Specials are those dogs that have already acquired a champion title. The best of males and best of females compete against those specials for the "best of breed" title, and among the best of male and female for the "best of winners" title. Best of breed is awarded at the end of the breed competition, along with best of opposite (sex) and best of winners.

Although many purebred dogs are shown by owners, many other owners don't have the time to travel every weekend in search of championship points and other awards, so they hire professional handlers to do the job for them. Handlers know how to present the dog to the best of its advantage, and they know how to hide faults, so if a client really wants to win, hiring a handler just makes sense. The main difference between an owner/handler and a professional is that the pro knows how to get a dog back on track when it isn't performing its best. Handlers may travel with a dozen dogs of the same breed and enter shows most weekends.

Hiring a handler doesn't come cheap. Handling expenses for showing three or four champion dogs may cost at least $150,000 a year. Very wealthy clients with the drive to be the best may spend up to $750,000 to hire an exclusive top handler, hire private jets to get the dogs to more shows, and so on. Clients pay a handler to take the dog in the ring, and if the dog wins best of breed, a group placement, or best in show, the handler gets a bonus. The client also helps pay travel expenses and a board fee for the dog while it lives in the handler's kennel. Out of this money, the handler pays assistants, kennel expenses, meals, motel fees, motor home upkeep, and all other business expenses—before drawing a salary. Dogs who make it all the way to the top show in the country—Westminster—have been entered in many competitions at great expense,

sometimes spending hundreds of thousands of dollars. This is why some dogs are owned by consortiums, since it may take four or five people to pay for the dog.

A typical day in a handler's life begins early, with feeding and grooming. Handlers work with their dogs every day to keep them in top physical and mental condition, to keep their coats healthy, and to teach them to stand and gait for the judge. Each dog gets only about two minutes in front of the judge, so a handler needs to make sure that for those two minutes, the dog's very best aspects are revealed.

The handler spends lots of time grooming the dog to perfection, but his or her own outfit must also be just right. Most handlers try to dress as if they were going to a job interview or giving a speech in front of a large group of people. You'll want to look as good as possible when you appear as a handler. Most of these professionals wear a plain outfit so as not to distract from the dog; this means you'll need to forget the wild Hawaiian prints, frills, florals, and big dots. Dress conservatively, and make sure you're not the same color as your dog. If your dog's coat is black, for example, you might want to wear white. Make sure your hair is neatly brushed.

As a dog show judge checks out the dog, the handler must try to keep the dog as still as possible and facing forward. (Puppies may wiggle a bit, which is understandable, as long as he or she is wiggling because she's a puppy and not shy or fearful.) Sometimes judges will ask the handler to show the dog's bite, but often they will examine it themselves.

Once judging for the handler's breed is over, that's it for the day, unless the dog took "best of breed" and will be in group competition. Group competition is optional, but it's not a good idea to skip the group

Peter Green, dog handler

In the insular world of dog showing, Peter Green is one of the best-known handlers in the world. Tied for most "best in show" records at Westminster, the dogs he has handled have won the coveted Best in Show four times: in 1968, 1977, 1994, and 1998. "I've been very successful at Westminster," he says modestly. "I've been going since 1960. I'm going back every year, but after this year I won't be handling." Instead, he will continue to breed terriers and he's thinking of starting to judge.

"I always said the reason I'm a handler is because I can't afford to show my own dogs," he says. "To be a good dog handler, you have to really like dogs, because you'll be around them 24 hours a day. You're on the job every day."

In addition to handling, Green breeds terriers, explaining that specializing in terriers is a tough job. It takes years to become proficient just in trimming the little dogs. To breed and handle terriers, "you have to be really dedicated, because it takes so much time to get these dogs into condition." He's also the coauthor of *New Secrets of Successful Dog Show Handling*, with Mario Migliorini.

Starting out, most handlers specialize in one type of dog, he explains. "You have people who specialize in sporting dogs, people who specialize in poodles, spaniels, working breeds . . . then they branch out into other groups, but usually they start in one branch of the field, and as they get more knowledge, they branch out into other breeds."

Green was raised in Wales, where he got his start working with dogs with an uncle. After he became a dog handler in Britain, he came to the United States to manage a kennel for a client and show their dogs. "Then I went into business showing dogs for anybody who wanted to pay me," he says.

If you're interested in becoming a handler someday, you can begin quite young, Green says. "Junior showmanship is a big thing in the United States," he says. "These kids get involved when they're very young. Then, if they really have a passion for it—which is what it takes—they usually go

competition if the judge who awarded your dog best of breed that day is also judging the group. "Best in show" competition is mandatory for group winners.

Once back home, the handler must take care of the dogs and then think about what went right and what went wrong, and how things could improve. Some handlers keep a journal for this purpose.

Pitfalls

Handling dogs is hard work, and it's very hard to make a good living. There's a lot more to competitions than parading a dog in front of a judge. You're up at 5 a.m. feeding and exercising the dogs, constantly walking and grooming, and lugging crates at shows. The work can be exhausting, with hours of driving to shows, loading and unloading equipment, grooming and showing, and subsisting on drive-through meals. It's a 24-hour, seven-day-a-week job, so if you're going to do it, you have to love it. And the money, for most handlers, is very small; many handlers say you can't make a living at it unless you're a top-rated handler. It can be a stressful business; if you don't win, you get fired.

Perks

If you love dogs and find dog shows intoxicating, this could be the life for you.

and work for an established dog handler, sometimes while they're still in school." If they get very serious about the job, he says, they then go to work for themselves full time.

It may sound like fun, working and playing with dogs all day, but Green is quick to correct that idea. "It's not an easy business," he says. "There are not many handlers in the United States, and we all work under American Kennel Club rules and regulations. We were just on the circuit in Florida, which had twenty-some shows, and people came from all over the U.S. You're working literally from 6 in the morning until 9:30 at night. Dogs take a lot of taking care of. It's not easy work, it's hard work for what you get paid. But it's a passion. It's something people love—they love their dogs, they like the competition.

"Dogs rely on you for everything," he says. "They're the most loving creatures there are. Everything you say to them, they understand. You can get very emotionally involved."

At times Green and his staff may be handling 40 dogs. "We have a crew of four handlers when we go to a show, with another four helpers. It's a lot of work and organization."

Yet as hard a job as dog handling can be, it's something Peter Green loves to do. "There's nothing about the job I don't like," he says. "The dog world is a separate world, with enthusiasts all over the world. When I was young, it used to be that to go to Europe was a big thing. Nowadays the world's so small, and with the Internet, everybody knows everybody in the world. Dogs who are winning in Australia or winning in Argentina, people all over know about it."

It may sound glamorous, traveling to shows all over the country, but when you get there you've got to work the whole time, Green explains. "We go to dog shows all over the U.S., but the only thing we see is the dog show, the arena. That's where we spend our time. It's not a glamorous job, it's a hard-work job, but there's a great deal of satisfaction in it . . . trying to get the terriers to look better than my competitors' dogs. When you win, you have the satisfaction of making a dog look as good as it can look, having your peers say: 'Yeah, it's really as good as you say it is.'"

Many handlers are second or third-generation dog enthusiasts. It may not be glamorous, but it's the thrill of victory that keeps people on the circuit.

Get a Jump on the Job

If you love dogs and want to learn more about handling them, you can approach a handler to see if he or she needs an assistant. Some breeders will arrange for a responsible teenager to borrow a dog for American Kennel Club (AKC) junior handling competition. Talk to as many handlers as you can (but not as they are preparing their dogs at a show; they won't want to be distracted). Read about the subject (see "Read More About It" at the back of this book). You can join e-mail groups dedicated to the dog handling scene. And there's nothing like observing the real thing: go sit by the ring at a show for a couple of hours and watch handlers at work, and take notes so you can remember what you've seen later. You can learn as much from a bad handler as you can from a good handler, so pay attention to everything. Think about working with someone who is prepared to mentor you.

DOG SHOW JUDGE

OVERVIEW

It looks like an impossible job: striding up and down a ring, watching a group of beautiful dogs that, to the casual observer, all look like perfectly gorgeous, perfect examples of the breed. And yet within a few heart-stopping seconds, the judge must point out the top three or four winners, and it's all over.

Being a dog show judge takes composure, a great eye for a good dog, and a solid knowledge of the breed being judged. Depending on the size of the show, there might be one judge for all breeds and classes, or, at larger dog shows, as many as 10 judges working in the rings. Dogs at shows are grouped in seven categories of breed: sporting, hound, working, terriers, toy, nonsporting, and herding.

To be a top dog show judge, you need to know a lot more than that you just love dogs. A judge needs to know a lot about dogs in general and certain breeds in particular, gleaned over the years by breeding dogs and learning to recognize the qualities that make a champion in one or two breeds. Many breeders who want to be judges also handle dogs of several breeds so they learn about others besides their own. It's not something you can learn in a couple of classes.

To prepare to judge a breed takes a lot of study, including attending seminars, ringside mentoring from top people in the breed, and visiting and speaking with many breeders. Judges also need to learn how things work at dog shows, so prospective judges

typically first volunteer to serve on show committees and act as stewards for working judges. (Stewards help the judge by handing armbands to competitors, calling dogs into the ring in proper order, and making sure the ribbons and prizes are ready when the judge needs them.) Applicants must have served as a ring steward at least six times. They practice judging at matches for

---

AT A GLANCE

Salary Range

Judges earn a small fee along with travel expenses, but they usually have regular day jobs or have a retirement income.

Education/Experience

Although there are no university requirements to be a dog show judge, the vast majority of judges have had to pass a difficult exam, along with other hurdles, to become a judge.

Personal Attributes

Dog show judges should be patient, fair, honest, calm, and able to make quick decisions.

Requirements

Licensure as a dog judge is required, granted by either a breed association or a kennel club. The license might either show the range of breeds that the individual is able to judge, or otherwise any exclusions. To be a judge, you'll need to have spent at least 12 years showing dogs, working at dog shows, and breeding dogs, and have bred and raised at least five litters from one breed, with at least four champions from those litters. Becoming a judge requires a detailed knowledge of not only breed standards, but canine anatomy and physiology as well.

Outlook

Fair. Although dog shows continue to be popular, there is little stability in the dog show world.

Skip Stanbridge, dog show judge

For the past 30 years, Skip Stanbridge has been a fixture in show rings throughout the world. An Ontario breeder of Belgian sheepdogs and owner of Mi-Sha-Ook kennels, he's licensed in Canada to judge all breeds of dogs in all seven groups—sporting, hounds, working, terriers, toys, non-sporting, and herding dogs. His judging skills have taken him throughout Canada and to all parts of the world, to dog shows in Argentina, Australia, Belgium, Brazil, Chile, Colombia, Costa Rica, Denmark, England, Estonia, Finland, France, Holland, Israel, Mexico, New Zealand, Norway, Peru, Sweden, the United States, and Venezuela.

It all started with one pet dog. "My wife and I have been married for 47 years," he says, "and the year after we were married we bought a dog." After they got that first dog, they began to show, and then to breed. From there, it was only a matter of time before Stanbridge moved on into judging. "I progressed through the judging ranks," he says. "It was a natural progression. To become a judge in North America, you have to have gone through the breeder and exhibitor stage. You can't just decide tomorrow to be a dog show judge." Stanbridge explains that both the American Kennel Club and the Canadian Kennel Club require that all judges spend a certain amount of time breeding and showing dogs.

Although Stanbridge breeds Belgian shepherds, he's an all-breed judge. "There are judges who judge only one breed, some who judge multiple breeds, and then some who judge three or four groups. I judge all breeds in all seven groups."

To become a judge, he says, you have to like dogs. "You have to have a fascination with dogs, but beyond that there's an aesthetic aspect to it. There's a certain excitement about a dog who's built correctly and has a certain look, who conforms to the standard, but who is also able to go out in the ring to show himself off." But there's more, Stanbridge explains. "There's also the understanding that behind all of that, there is some very hard work in developing a breeding program. Judges appreciate the fact that truly great dogs don't come about by accident. It takes a lot of hard work on the part of owners, breeders, and handlers."

But liking dogs is only part of the package. "You basically have to like people, too," Stanbridge says, "because you're dealing with people all the time. After all, 90 percent of the people in the ring lose. The more you enjoy that aspect of the job, the more exhibitors are prepared to enjoy the experience as well."

That being said, judging dogs for a living just doesn't pay that much, and neither does dog breeding. "I don't think anyone makes a living judging dogs," Stanbridge says. "A very few of the serious dog breeders do make a living, but very few dog breeders do. Most of us support our breeding habit by working elsewhere. Some judges supplement their retirement income through judging, but it would be very difficult to make a living judging dogs. In fact, it would be almost impossible." Stanbridge supported his breeding habit by teaching at a local university; he's a former university dean and vice president of Mohawk College in Hamilton, Ontario.

Of course, the world of show dogs is very small, and inevitably there are questions about fairness. "You're not allowed to judge your own dogs or members of your family," Stanbridge says. "Someone who has your line may exhibit under you, but that does raise some questions," he says. "But most serious dog people who understand what goes on understand that judges try very

(continues)

(continued)

hard to put up the best dog. There's always those who will find reasons for why their dog lost, and part of that may be: 'The judge knows that dog or exhibitor.'"

The only thing Stanbridge doesn't really enjoy about judging is the travel. "Most judges will tell you today that travel is really becoming very burdensome between lineups and security checks," he says, "and most clubs who employ you expect you to fly the cheapest way possible." And sometimes, judges find themselves asked to judge a group of dogs who just aren't very good. "If you run into a bunch of dogs who aren't particularly good, you find yourself wondering what you're doing. You ask yourself: 'Why am I spending the afternoon sorting these dogs who aren't that good?' But then a great one comes in and you get all excited again."

When he first started judging, he enjoyed the idea of travel. "But after about 30 years of running around the world, travel ceases to become as exciting or as motivating as it once was."

If you love dogs and dream someday of judging a ringful of canines, Stanbridge advises you to make sure you love what you're doing. "In order for people to truly do a good job, they have to enjoy dogs, enjoy the whole competitive nature of the dog show game.

"I try to draw a similarity between teaching and judging," he says. "Teaching is a wonderful profession as long as you enjoy doing it. It's a horrendous profession if you don't enjoy it. The same is true for dog show judging. I'm not saying that everything goes along wonderfully well every day, but if you truly enjoy the process, it's a wonderful, rewarding thing to do."

And it's something Stanbridge figures he'll continue to do for the foreseeable future. "As long as I've got legs to carry me and a brain that continues to function reasonably well, I hope to keep judging a few more years," he says. "It becomes a question of regulating yourself—when do you get tired of the game? People pay an awful lot of money to show dogs, so judges have an obligation to make sure people are getting their money's worth. They have an obligation to give their honest and informed opinions."

puppies and inexperienced dogs, but don't award points towards championships. The applicant also must watch the AKC video of each breed they want to judge, and pass an "open book" exam on anatomy.

Once you've learned a lot about your breed, you can apply to the American Kennel Club for approval to be a judge of your breed. Anyone in good standing with the AKC can apply to be a judge, but to be eligible, you'll need to comply with the 12-5-4 rule—that is, spent at least 12 years showing dogs, working at dog shows, and breeding dogs. You'll also need to have bred and raised at least 5 litters from one breed, and produced at least 4 champions from those litters. In order to be able to judge other breeds, you have to study, do more match assignments, and attend seminars with people who know a lot about each breed. All kinds of people apply to be judges, including lawyers, doctors, veterinarians, dentists, psychologists, professors, groomers and kennel owners, and former professional handlers.

Some people aren't allowed to be judges, including current professional handlers or members of their household, AKC employees, people in the dog food or dog equipment business, for-profit dog breeders or brokers, and anyone connected with dog magazines or publications that may solicit advertising. Beyond that, any qualified person is eligible.

Applications are sent to the AKC and the name and address of the applicant, as well as the breeds applied for, are published in the *AKC Gazette*. The applicant is interviewed by an AKC representative and the application is reviewed by the Judges' Committee and Board of Directors. If approved, the applicant is granted provisional status for the approved breeds, and another notice will appear in the *Gazette* stating that the individual—now called a *provisional judge*—is now approved. At this point, the judge may accept assignments, but they have to pay for their own airfare and hotel, and earn just a flat rate of $3 per dog in their assignment. A provisional judge must complete five assignments in each breed requested; after this, the judge can apply for regular status.

If no complaints about the judge have been filed with the AKC by this time, a third note is made in the *Gazette* stating that provisional assignments are completed and that the judge is now finally approved for the breeds listed. After a year, a judge may apply for more breeds, but no more than the number for which they've already been approved. They may have experience owning, breeding, and raising these breeds, but more often the judge can qualify to apply by attending regional or national specialties of those breeds, attending breed seminars put on by national-club representatives and AKC institutes, judging sweepstakes and matches, or by observing in the ring a long-time judge of that breed.

Eventually, a judge may continue to pick up breeds until he or she is approved for all breeds within one of the seven variety groups. The judge is now eligible to judge not only all the breeds in the group, but the group competition as well. When a judge has successfully completed five assignments judging a Variety Group, they are now eligible to judge Best in Show. Judges may also branch out into other groups and pick up all the breeds in those as well. A few judges, about 20 or so of the nearly 3,000 AKC-licensed conformation judges, are eligible to judge all 150-odd AKC approved breeds.

A judge assesses the breed by using a sort of blueprint for canine perfection, called the *breed standard*—a set of written rules about how the breed should look, which are written and owned by the parent clubs of each breed. Most standards describe the dog's general appearance, movement, temperament, and specific physical traits such as height and weight, coat, colors, eye color and shape, ear shape and placement, feet, and tail. Some standards can be very specific, but others are more general and leave room for individual interpretation. Using this standard, dogs aren't really judged against each other. Instead, they're judged by how closely they meet the standard. This is why dogs of different breeds can be judged beside each other. A judge must not only really know the breed standards, but must be able to apply those standards in a heartbeat for each dog being judged.

No prospective judge may apply for more than 13 breeds at a time. First-time applicants will usually be given one or two breeds to judge, while former professional handlers may receive more. At some larger shows, a judge may see as many as 175 dogs a day, taking only a few minutes with each animal.

Pitfalls

It can take a very long time to become experienced enough to confidently judge a dog show, and the pay is quite low for the time invested. Dog show judging can be highly political and therefore there are a lot of egos and personalities to deal with.

Perks

People who love dogs, specific breeds, and dog shows thrive on the atmosphere and excitement of a top dog show. As the judge, you're the central player in this exciting drama, and many judges really love what they do and find it personally fulfilling.

Get a Jump on the Job

If you love dogs and are interested in shows, read as much as you can about various breeds and attend dog shows. Even young people can handle a dog in a show, so work with your own dog if you have one. If you don't, see if you can volunteer with a kennel near your home or help a handler.

DUDE RANCHER

OVERVIEW

Ropin', ridin', and ranchin'—you'll find it all at a dude ranch, which aims to bring the western experience to vacationing families out to have a good time. One thing that all hands-on dude ranchers have in common is that they're hard workers. Most dude ranchers love what they do, but not one of them would say their job is an easy one.

Most dude ranches are working ranches, where guests are invited to stay and experience a lifestyle that is very different from the typical workaday world. Activities offered vary from ranch to ranch, but horseback riding is a must. Most dude ranches offer several trail rides a day, with some providing the opportunity for overnight rides and other adventures. Other activities a dude rancher may offer to guests include fishing, helping with ranch animals, hiking, square dances, hay rides, and game or movie nights.

Most dude ranches operate seasonally and offer stays of one week or more. Some dude ranches are fairly basic, offering comfortable but simple accommodations with three meals served in the mess hall each day. Others offer whirlpools, a full range of spa services, and gourmet dining served in fancy surroundings. As a dude ranch owner, it's up to you to decide what type of facility you'll offer, based on research into current trends and preferences, cost, competition, and personal preferences.

Someone with prior hotel or restaurant experience, for instance, may want to capitalize on that by offering a variety of amenities for guests. A family opening their ranch to guests in order to boost its income, however, might be more inclined

to offer comfortable, no-frills accommodations and simple activities. Some ranches become dude ranches out of economic

Emer and Aleesa Wiltbank, dude ranchers

The eastern part of Arizona is home to Emer and Aleesa Wiltbank, owners of Sprucedale, an Arizona dude ranch that's been in Emer's family for three generations. When Emer's grandfather bought the property in Alpine, Arizona, in 1941 to raise his cattle and horses, there were a few small cabins on the property where friends and family members would stay when they visited. This gave Emer's grandmother the idea to build some more cabins and open the ranch to guests. This working ranch has been operating as a dude ranch ever since.

Today the ranch includes 15 cabins and a main lodge that accommodates 70 to 80 guests at a time from all over the United States and other countries, who come from Memorial Day through October. "We have families that have been coming back here for generations," Aleesa says. "People enjoy the simple life away from the city, phones, TV, and technology. They want to spend time with their families and remember what is important. We provide that experience."

While Sprucedale is not what you'd call luxurious, it does offer many comforts and opportunities for guests. The staff is up at 6 a.m., and any guest can help milk cows at 6:30 a.m. Breakfast is served from 7:45 a.m. until 8:15 a.m., and the first horseback ride of the day—a two-hour trail ride—sets out at 9:30 a.m. Lunch is served at 1 p.m., followed by an afternoon ride or other activities.

Dinner is served at 7 p.m., followed by an evening activity such as a bonfire, hayride, or square dance. Guests also can fish in the nearby Black River, join in a softball or volleyball game, hike, relax, read on their cabin porches, or simply enjoy the surrounding scenery.

Although guests can pick and choose their activities, the Wiltbanks and their staff are on the go from 6 a.m. until 10 at night. "The wranglers are training and riding horses; teaching guests horsemanship skills; and feeding the pigs, cows, chickens, and other various animals," Aleesa says. "There are cabins and vehicles to maintain, and pretty much a lot of physical work. The kitchen help is cooking and cleaning all day. We prepare all three meals and serve them family-style in our main house. We have laundry and up-keep of our own to do." When the Wiltbanks close up the ranch in November, they round up their daughter and all of their animals, and head to their winter home in Eagar, which is about an hour down the mountain. The ranch is uninhabitable in the harsh winter months because the roads are not maintained and their buildings are not winterized. As soon as the snow has melted enough for the roads to become passable again, however, they climb back up the mountain to begin preparing the ranch for another season of guests.

"It's a lot of hard work," Aleesa says, "but it is also a lot of fun."

necessity, while others start out as dude ranches.

Although most dude ranches are concentrated in the western part of the United States, you can find a few in the Smoky Mountains of North Carolina and Tennessee, as well as in a few eastern states. One dude ranch is located about 95 miles north of New York City in the Catskill and Shawangunk mountains of New York.

Owning and operating a dude ranch sounds like a great job, but it's not without its challenges. If you happen to be a member of family who owns a ranch, you've certainly got an advantage over someone who has to buy one. Dude ranches currently for sale cost about $1.5 million on up, according to the Wyoming-based Dude Ranchers Association. In addition to the cost, it can be difficult to get permits for your guests to ride on adjoining lands. Then there are the business considerations such as insurance, taxes, payroll, employee benefits, and so forth.

If you don't have the cash—or the nerve—to buy a dude ranch, you might want to think about becoming a dude ranch manager instead. Some owners hire full-time workers to manage their ranches. Managing a ranch allows you to have the western lifestyle without the financial burden.

Pitfalls

In addition to a very significant financial investment to get a ranch up and running, you should expect to wait from five to seven years before showing a profit. Ranchers of all sorts are subject to government restrictions and laws concerning land use, grazing rights, and other issues, so you must be prepared to keep informed about applicable legislation. As with owning any business, you'll need to deal with matters such as insurance, taxes, inventory, cash flow, accounts, and so forth, while making sure animals and guests are cared for and happy.

Perks

For most ranchers, the job is more than a career—it's a way of life that's satisfying and rewarding. If you love to be outdoors, work with animals, and you enjoy meeting new people, you'll love the dude ranch life.

Get a Jump on the Job

Some dude ranches offer summer jobs or internships to teens under age 18. Check out the Web site of the Dude Ranchers Association (http://www.duderanch.org) for employment and internship opportunities, or check out the Web sites of individual ranches that may be located near you. If you think dude ranching is in your future, work with your guidance counselor to determine a course of study, as you'll need both animal husbandry and business skills to be successful.

EQUINE DENTIST

OVERVIEW

A human's teeth are fairly predictable: You get one set as a toddler, you lose those baby teeth, and then you get another set. If you take good care of your teeth and you don't get whacked in the face with a softball, your teeth should remain pretty much as they are in your mouth throughout your adult years.

A horse's teeth, however, are altogether different. Horses get two sets of teeth, but those teeth continue to grow and change throughout the animal's life. They have very deep roots, and most of each tooth is located deep inside the jaw bone. Often, their teeth don't line up well enough for them to grow properly, or they don't come in contact with other teeth so as to prevent continued growth. When a horse's tooth doesn't grind against another one, it continues to develop a hook or point that can be extremely painful.

If a horse's teeth are left untreated, it can have serious health consequences to the animal. It could become unable to eat efficiently, which results in weight loss and other health problems. If the condition is painful, as it often can be, a horse may balk at having a bit put into its mouth and become difficult or impossible to ride. Even some cases of lameness are blamed on tooth problems, because the horse tries to compensate for mouth pain by changing its gait.

Fortunately, equine dentists can help keep horses healthy and comfortable by caring for their teeth and preventing problems from occurring or becoming serious.

AT A GLANCE

Salary Range

Salaries can vary greatly, depending on the number of customers and location. The average salary ranges from $40,000 and $70,000 a year.

Education/Experience

Most states require an equine dentist to be a veterinarian, with both an undergraduate degree and a degree from a college of veterinary medicine. However, there is ongoing discussion and legislative debate concerning the possibility of allowing practitioners trained in equine dentistry but who aren't veterinarians to become horse dentists.

Personal Attributes

You should be comfortable with and enjoy being around horses. Equine dentistry requires a fair amount of strength, and you should be in reasonably good physical condition. You also must be motivated and willing to establish contact and follow up with clients, and have a neat appearance.

Requirements

Equine dentists must be licensed veterinarians and must retain their licensing by completing ongoing professional education courses. Other requirements vary from state to state.

Outlook

There is an increasing awareness of the need for equine dentists. As horse owners become better educated about the advantages of proper dental care for their animals, the demand for equine dentists should continue to increase. In addition, horse owners are becoming more and more willing to spend more money on their mounts, and are paying for veterinary services that were not common in the past.

A thorough dental examination normally begins with an evaluation of the horse's overall health and condition. The equine dentist often sedates the animal in order

Tom Allen, equine dentist

Tom Allen is a Missouri-based veterinarian who spends much of his time on the road, tending to the dental needs of horses. Licensed in Missouri and five other states, he also works by veterinary referral in other locations.

Allen graduated from veterinary school in 1973, and was exposed to horse dentistry in the mid-1990s. The practice of equine dentistry caught his attention, and he began focusing more and more on learning the process and tending to horses' teeth. In the late 1990s he decided to limit his veterinary practice to equine dentistry. Since then, he's written several books on the practice, and has become well known as a speaker and educator.

He's adamant that equine dentistry is absolutely necessary to the health of the animal. "Many horses die prematurely due to untreated dental problems," Allen says. "Contrary to most veterinarian's current opinion, horses with even severe pathology in their mouths will not show significant symptoms. You have to perform a thorough examination to determine what's going on with their dental health."

Allen travels extensively to meet the needs of his four-footed clients. He tries to cluster appointments by location, and has several people bring their horses to one location for treatment. He travels with a specially designed dental trailer, in which the horse's teeth can be examined and the necessary treatment administered. An examination and treatment—including getting the horse into and out of the trailer, sedation, dental charting, performing any necessary procedures, and the reversal of sedation—normally takes about 45 minutes.

The most common necessary procedure, Allen says, is the removal of sharp points from the outside edges of the teeth along the horse's upper cheek. If not removed, these points cut into the horse's mouth, causing significant discomfort. He also rounds teeth to remove sharp edges from other teeth, and checks for infected teeth or malocclusions (incorrect biting or chewing positions).

Allen is amazed that a horse can have a severe dental problem without exhibiting any symptoms. "Some of these horses have had multiple teeth that were loose and wallowing in a pocket of pus," he says. "These teeth had to be painful to the horse, and yet no outward signs were evident."

Allen is a proponent of allowing well trained, non-veterinarians perform equine dentistry. For now, however, he advises anyone interested in the career to work toward becoming a veterinarian. With luck, Allen says, the demand for equine dentists will force legislators to change veterinary practice acts to allow non-veterinarians to become trained and certified to practice. If that should happen, someone with a background in animal science or a related field could learn horse dentistry at an institution such as The Academy of Equine Dentistry in Glenns Ferry, Idaho.

Allen is frustrated by the inability of non-veterinarians to become equine dentists, because there is a need for good people in the field in order to properly care for all the horses. He finds personal satisfaction in his work, and urges anyone interested to consider the career.

"Every horse that I work on now has a good chance of living longer, being able to perform better, eat more efficiently, and just be more comfortable in general. It's a good feeling to be able to provide such service."

to be able to work on its mouth. After the dentist checks the front teeth and evaluates the animal's bite, it's time to insert a full mouth speculum, which holds the horse's mouth open and allows the dentist to reach all of the teeth.

Using special hand and/or power tools, the dentist grinds down very long teeth; smoothes out sharp, pointed teeth; snips off any hooks; and otherwise improves the condition of the horse's mouth. Sometimes the dentist will extract a tooth that is infected. Each tooth in the horse's mouth should be evaluated, and treated if necessary.

It takes special training and a fair amount of nerve to work on a horse's mouth, even if the animal is sedated and docile.

Although equine dentistry is sometimes treated as if it's a new field, it's actually an old field that's gaining new attention. When people depended on horses for transportation and farming, they paid close attention to their teeth because a horse wouldn't work well if its mouth hurt. As the dependence on horses subsided, so did our interest in their oral health. It's easy to ignore a horse's teeth, because they often will exhibit few symptoms, even if the problems are severe.

Today, modern horse owners are being educated on the importance of dental care for their animals, and are showing increased interest in maintaining oral health. This will increase the need for horse dentists, which is why there is a movement underway to allow dental technicians to do the work that only veterinarians are permitted to do in most states.

Pitfalls

At the moment, you'll need to be licensed as a veterinarian in order to practice equine dentistry, which means you're in for years of schooling and a significant financial commitment. Equine dentistry requires some specialized equipment, which can be dauntingly expensive to buy all at once. Since most equine dentists are self-employed, you'll need to cover your own insurance policies and other expenses.

Perks

Equine dentists understand that they are providing a valuable service to horses and their owners, and gain much satisfaction from that. Because you normally go to the horse, you get to spend time traveling and be outside instead of confined to an office. You'll meet a lot of horse owners who share similar interests, and get to hang out with some beautiful animals, as well. Once you're established as an equine dentist, you can manage your schedule to suit you.

Get a Jump on the Job

Prepare yourself for college by taking all the science, math, and biology courses that you can in middle school and high school. Try to get a job working in a veterinarian's office, stable, or other facility where you'll come in contact with horses, as veterinary schools are more likely to accept applicants who have experience working with animals. Read all you can about equine dentistry, and spend as much time as you can around horses, even if it means you need to trade stable cleaning services for riding privileges.

EXOTIC ANIMAL VETERINARIAN

OVERVIEW

If a giraffe gets a sore throat or a hippo has a toothache, it takes a very special kind of vet to figure out what's wrong. An exotic animal veterinarian provides care for animals other than the dogs and cats that other veterinarians treat. Exotic animals include everything from boa constrictors to parrots and guinea pigs.

Most courses in veterinary school include an overview of different animals including marine animals and wildlife, but most courses are specific to domestic companion pets and farm animals. Birds and reptiles are included to a lesser degree, but the more exotic animals require specialization in aquatic medicine and wild animal medicine. This is why general vets may have a basic knowledge of exotic animal physiology, but they don't have the experience, special equipment, or specific medicines to treat them.

As exotic pets become increasingly popular for regular people to adopt, the veterinarians who treat them will need to continue learning about different species of animals, their habits and habitats, and health problems. Exotic animal veterinarians see animals due for regular checkups, as well as those that are sick or have been injured. Emergency care sometimes is necessary, which means you'd have to juggle other appointments in order to take care of the animal requiring immediate attention.

Exotic animals often require care quite different from what you'd find in a typical dog and cat hospital. An iguana, for instance, needs to have a heat source. And

AT A GLANCE

Salary Range

The average salary for an exotic animal veterinarian is about $65,000 a year, according to government statistics. The lowest 10 percent earned less than $39,000, and the highest 10 percent were paid more than $124,000.

Education/Experience

Becoming a veterinarian of any sort requires a lot of education. You'll need a four-year undergraduate degree, preferably in animal science, biology, zoology, or a related field. You'll also need to earn a Doctor of Veterinary Medicine (D.V.M. or V.M.D.) degree from an accredited school before you can begin practicing.

Personal Attributes

In addition to a liking for animals and interest in helping them when they are sick or injured, you also will need the ability to get along with pet owners, who often are passionate about their animals. You should be compassionate, and yet able to detach yourself from your work. If you plan to establish your own practice, you should be somewhat business oriented unless you can afford to hire someone to manage the practice. You also should have the ability to pay attention to detail, to make sound decisions quickly, and to be able to work on your own.

Requirements

All states require veterinarians to be licensed before they start practicing. Licensing requirements vary from state to state, but all states require that the applicant has passed a national board examination and has a D.V.M. degree. Most states also require applicants to pass a state exam that covers state laws and regulations, and some states require further testing on clinical competency. In addition, most states require veterinarians to take continuing education courses to keep up with many new techniques, ideas, and recent diseases.

(continues)

AT A GLANCE *(continued)*

Outlook

Very good. Jobs for all veterinarians, including exotic animal vets, are expected to increase faster than average between now and 2012. This is attributed to several factors, including the fact that pet owners are becoming increasingly willing to spend money on their pets, and are paying for veterinary services that were not common in the past. Veterinary practices that treat exotic animals are one of the fastest growing segments of the veterinary field.

because exotic animals often aren't domesticated, they could be dangerous if not handled correctly.

If you're interested in exotic animal medicine, you may be able to find that some veterinary schools offer courses or clinics in exotic animal medicine, although few offer training in primate medicine. This experience must be obtained by doing extra projects and/or summer jobs with a primate center or zoo, attending conferences, and through externships at primate facilities. There are 28 colleges and universities in the United States that are accredited by the Council on Education of the American Veterinary Association. The D.V.M. degree is a four-year program. If you seek board certification in exotic small-animal medicine, you must also complete a three- to four-year residency program that provides intensive training in this field.

After vet school, you have several options for more training. Internships in zoo animal medicine are generally required for the next phase of veterinary training, which is a residency program in exotic or zoo animal medicine. Vets may become board certified in zoo animal medicine,

much like medical doctors do in their specialty fields, by meeting specific training and publishing requirements and passing a rigorous test.

Several organizations offer annual conferences and helpful Web sites, including the American Association of Zoo Veterinarians (http://www.aazv.org), the Association for Primate Veterinarians, and the American Association of Laboratory Animal Scientists (http://www.aalas.org).

It's important for exotic animal veterinarians to keep up with advances in exotic medicine and surgery. Exotic animal medicine is an evolving field, and there is much to learn. Diligent exotic animal vets attend conferences and roundtable discussions to learn about and share information concerning new issues and techniques. Continuing education is required for all veterinarians, and an increasing number of courses targeted at exotic animal vets are becoming available.

Pitfalls

Being an exotic animal veterinarian requires years of study and a lifetime of dedication to your work. While it's sure to be interesting, the work can be difficult and tedious, requiring extensive knowledge and the ability to put that knowledge to use by making life-or-death decisions concerning your animal patients. Another negative for some people is the business end of the job. Private clinical practice can be especially stressful because of the investment in equipment and medicine, and the responsibility for employees.

Perks

Every day will be different as an exotic animal veterinarian, and you're sure to meet a lot of interesting pets and their owners. Veterinarians with established practices

Jose Biascoechea, exotic animal veterinarian

If it's not a dog, a cat, or a farm animal, Jose Biascoechea will treat it. An exotic animal veterinarian in Mount Pleasant, South Carolina, his practice is growing due to the increasing number of exotic pets and demand for their care. He's treated frogs, fish, turtles, tortoises, guinea pigs, rats, hamsters, iguanas, bearded dragons, hedgehogs, parrots, and macaws in his line of work. Biascoechea, who has an undergraduate degree in biology and a doctorate of veterinary medicine from Kansas State University, enjoys the fact that no two days are alike.

"There are no typical days," he says. "On any given day I have 10 scheduled appointments, including wellness visits as well as sick animal appointments. But you never know if there is going to be an emergency situation."

The world of exotic animals is strange, and Biascoechea sometimes has to play the role of detective to figure out what's going on with a creature. That's what he had to do when an owner brought in a lethargic tarantula, who hadn't eaten anything or moved for several days. Biascoechea could tell immediately that the tarantula's environment was too dry, so he placed the spider in a humidified, warm incubator. About an hour later when he went to check on the spider, Biascoechea saw that it had molted (shed its outer shell).

"The owners were not providing enough moisture in its environment, and the spider had effectively been trapped inside his own exoskeleton for several days," Biascoechea says.

Pet owners without sufficient knowledge to properly care for exotic animals are very common, Biascoechea says, and end up causing a lot of problems for their pets. "The biggest problem I face is clients who are not educated with regard to proper diet and husbandry of their exotic pets," he says. "I have to work hard to provide detailed care sheets informing the owner of the special needs of their pets."

For instance, he says, many people don't realize that rabbits and guinea pigs need to have a lot of fresh hay in their diets, to keep their teeth from growing too big. "When hay is not the bulk of the diet, the teeth can grow out of control and require filing or extraction," Biascoechea says.

Biascoechea warns that being an exotic veterinarian is not for everyone. In addition to needing smarts and sound resolve, you'll also need business skills in order to run your practice.

"This is not a career path for the squeamish or faint of heart, nor for those who need constant approval and support," Biascoechea says. "In most cases you are on your own, armed only with your skills and knowledge. Often you'll find that in addition to the veterinary training you receive in school, you'll also need a thorough knowledge of business practices, managerial skills, tax laws, and everything else related to running a small business."

can command quite a high salary, as people are willing to pay well for the care of their unusual pets.

Get a Jump on the Job

Volunteer or get a job at a pet store that sells exotic animals, a zoo, or in the office of an exotic animal veterinarian. Read everything that you can about exotic animals, and visit Web sites of veterinarians and veterinary organizations. Keep in mind that some veterinary medical colleges place a lot of emphasis on your veterinary and animal experience in deciding whether to admit you. Formal experience, such as work with veterinarians or scientists in clinics, agribusiness, research, or some area of health science, is of particular benefit to you. Less formal experience, such as working with animals on a farm or ranch or at a stable or animal shelter, also is helpful. Vet schools will be looking for students who demonstrate ambition and an eagerness to work with animals, so get as much experience as you can in working with animals before you go off to college.

FARRIER

OVERVIEW

To the casual observer, horseshoeing looks easy—you grab a hoof, yank off a shoe, and hammer on a new one. But in fact, the art of blacksmithing (or *farriery*) is physically challenging and so complex that the craft can take a lifetime to truly master.

There are three reasons why horses wear shoes: to protect their hooves, to give them traction, and to change the way they move. Protection is the most common reason why horses are shod. Without a shoe, a horse's hoof could wear down faster than his hoof could grow; this would cause soreness. Think how your finger feels if you accidentally clip your fingernail too short—it hurts. A horse's hoof is the same thing.

Horseshoes are typically made from rubber, plastic, steel, aluminum, or titanium. Steel is the most common material, since these horseshoes are readily available and easiest to use. They can be easily modified or forged from bar stock with only minimal forging, and come in a variety of widths, thicknesses, and configurations. In fact, many farriers never use anything other than steel shoes. Occasionally, however, some horses need other kinds of shoes.

Aluminum shoes are popular in horses used for flat and harness racing, and on the front feet of horses used for speed (such as in barrel racing) where weight of the shoe is an important factor. Aluminum is also very popular on the front hooves of horses used to hunt, since many trainers believe it improves the way a hunter moves. It's also the first choice of many veterinary farriers as its greater width and thickness can be used to protect sensitive parts of the foot without adding weight. However, aluminum

AT A GLANCE

Salary Range

A beginning farrier with six weeks of shoeing school earns about $24,000 a year; more experienced farriers may earn between $36,000 and $65,000 depending on experience, reputation, and education.

Education/Experience

Farriers need to have experience with horses, but there is no formal farrier training system. Although horseshoeing is an art, it is also a science. A background in the sciences (especially equine anatomy and physiology) becomes important when diagnosing, treating, and discussing foot ailments with a veterinarian. That's why many farriers seek formal training at a trade school, college, or university.

Personal Attributes

Farriers should be comfortable around horses and have above average mechanical ability, be independent and able to think for themselves, and have a strong, healthy body, because few jobs are so physically demanding. Farriers must work very quickly and be able to handle unpredictable or agitated horses. Farriers also must be courteous, polite, and tactful when dealing with people, and they should have good hand-eye coordination. Although most people think of blacksmiths as men because the work is so physically strenuous, today 10 percent of American Farriers Association–certified farriers are women.

Requirements

There is no farrier licensing or registration required, and certification programs offered by farrier associations are voluntary. The American Farriers Association (AFA) has taken the lead in providing certification exams for its members with credible standards; candidates must pass both practical and written tests. A successful professional farrier must thoroughly understand equine anatomy and care of the foot and have skills in horsemanship, forging,

(continues)

isn't quite as easy to forge or weld as steel. Solid rubber and plastic shoes are occasionally used to help treat pathological foot conditions. Titanium is sometimes used on big race horses or jumpers who need a light, very strong shoe in front.

Putting on a horseshoe involves a lot more than hammering metal onto a horse's hoof. First of all, each hoof is different, and a farrier needs to learn the best type of shoe and placement on the hoof for best performance. You've got to fit, make, or nail horseshoes (or in the case of race horses, racing plates or *tips*). You've also got to be able to analyze the shape and condition of the hoof, as well as what the horse will be used for, in order to make sure that you do the best possible job. Will the horse be a show jumper, needing much lighter aluminum shoes? Will the horse be racing, or simply used for trail riding? For racehorses, the farrier must remove steel shoes from each horse before a race, replacing them with light aluminum shoes or "tips"; after the race, the tips are replaced with steel shoes.

Because shoes also can be used to help correct some faults in a horse's stride or gait, a professional farrier should be able to spot these problems by looking at a horse's legs and hooves while the animal is standing still and in motion to check for irregularities, interference, odd gait, or abnormalities in size and shape of hooves. Farriers also may get involved with surgical shoeing, to correct hoof deformities.

At a typical shoeing, the farrier takes a good look at the horse, talks to the horse's owner or trainer to decide on the type of shoe required, and then removes the worn or faulty shoes, noting wear patterns and any foreign bodies, bruising, infections, or deformities in the hoof. The farrier then examines, cleans, trims, and shapes the hooves using a knife, hoof cutter, and a rasp. Then it's time to measure each hoof, making a template on a piece of cardboard and estimating the length of metal that will be needed for the shoes. The farrier then selects and cuts the metal according to type, size, and weight of the shoes, along with the right kind of nails, and holds the shoe against the hoof to assess the amount of shaping. Now it's on to the forge, as the farrier heats the shoe, shaping it on an anvil and hammering it to size. Once the shoe is made, the farrier places and nails the shoe to each hoof, checking that clips and clenched nails are smooth and lined up with the edges of each hoof.

Horseshoeing is much more than a 9-to-5 job. As a professional farrier, you'll be working closely with horse owners and vets to help keep horses healthy and in peak condition.

As you can imagine, learning how to do all these tasks isn't an easy job. In the past, farriers always apprenticed with a knowledgeable blacksmith to learn the trade, since horseshoeing is a craft best learned one on one. However, today there are very few opportunities to become an

Jeff Hyser, farrier

Jeff Hyser didn't grow up riding horses or thinking about shoeing horses for a living—in fact, he didn't really think about horses at all. "I never thought in my wildest dreams that I'd be a farrier," he says. But he did observe the benefits of self-employment; his dad owned his own business, driving a route for snack food sales.

Then in his early 30s, he rented a small farm, and his brother boarded some horses with him. "I said, 'Do you mind if I start riding?'" Hyser recalls, and before long he was hooked. He bought his own horse, and when the farrier arrived six months later, Hyser was intrigued. He rode with the farrier for about three months to see if he liked the job. Hyser found that he liked horses and he liked the farrier life, so off he went to four-week Oklahoma Horseshoeing School.

When he got back to his farm in York, Pennsylvania, he put an ad in the paper offering his services as farrier. "The first horse I did took me three hours to do something that now takes me a half hour," he says. "I was really struggling in the beginning. It took me five years to get full time." Just when he began to think that the job was really just too difficult to make a living, he met famed farrier Bob Kain in Lancaster, Pa. "I went down and met him, and he helped me and watched me. If I was out on a job and I had trouble, I would call him," he says. "I would ride with him [to his jobs] and he was really helpful. Without him, I would have quit. He never paid me, but it was worth it for me to learn from him. Some farriers will charge people to go along and observe, but Bob Kain was like a friend. He appreciated me helping because obviously he could do more horses that way."

Hyser, like many farriers, uses a fair amount of preformed horseshoes. "It would be nice if every horse's foot was exactly the same," he says, "but 9 out of 10 shoes, you've gotta bend. For a lame horse, I can make a custom shoe. But to sit there and make four shoes would take an hour. If you pull a shoe out of a box, you can be ready to go in five minutes. You can shape a stock shoe pretty quickly."

His route includes rural York and Lancaster counties. "I try to stay within an hour's driving distance," he explains. "That way, if a shoe would come off, it's not too far to drive. I keep closing my circle; my furthest customer is about 45 minutes away. As I get people closer and closer to my house, I can weed out the less desirable ones."

If you think you'd like to shoe horses for a living, Hyser recommends you ride along with another farrier for a few days to see if you really like the job. "There was another job I was going to do, delivering papers," he says. "I rode along with the guy for 10 minutes and said—'Forget this!' At farrier school, a couple of people were never around horses, and they'd come out with their clothes all tore up and bleeding. You need to get a feel for it to see if you'll like it."

If you do decide to set up shop as a farrier, you'll need to have money to buy the necessary tools. Hyser estimates that his tools are worth about $10,000, including a forge. "It probably took me one or two years to get all the tools I have now," he says. "Even a good pair of horse snippers is $150. When I went to school, I had to buy snippers, a box—it cost about $1,000 to start. Then when I got with Bob, he helped me out, sold me a used anvil."

You'll also need to be physically strong. "Some days are harder than others," he says. "Some days I might only work four or five hours. If I go to one place with 10 or 12 horses, afterwards

(continues)

(continued)

physically I'm shot. To work 10 or 12 hours a day, your back would wear out a lot faster. I try to keep it to 30 or 40 horses a week." The result, he says, is that after 10 years, he still feels good. But it doesn't take long for those muscles to get out of shape. "If I take a few days off and then go do a few horses, I feel it for a couple of days," he says.

Part of the job involves keeping current with new techniques. Hyser says there are farrier seminars all year long, and he keeps current by reading trade magazines. "If I run into a problem, there's a couple of farriers I can call. I think, 'What would Bob do?'"

Hyser figures that his freedom is his favorite part of the job. "I like the freedom. And if I do a good job, people appreciate it. Some give me a tip. Word gets around. Working for myself is the best part. If I want to take it easy, I can do that." Not that there aren't also a few negatives to being self-employed, he notes. "If I do something wrong I have to stand there and take it. I can't say: 'Hey, go call my boss.'"

His least favorite part of the job might be the occasional customer who just doesn't know much about horses. "I have trouble with people who own horses but who don't know how dangerous they are," he says. In the beginning, "anyone who couldn't get a farrier [because they owned a difficult horse] would call me . . . But now I have really good customers. People without the knowledge of horses don't understand that you need to correct a horse who acts up. If you don't, they'll just keep doing it.

"Today, I probably have 100 regular customers, and all of them are really good. After you get a good reputation, you show up on time, charge a reasonable price, you can weed out the bad.

"If I keep my philosophy of not overdoing it, I hope to keep doing it until I fall over. I know some farriers who are 75 years old. But I know some young guys working 12 hours a day, they even say they won't last at that rate. I've found something I like, and I'd like to do it until I'm 65 or 70, even if I'm only doing three or four horses. I consider my customers my friends."

apprentice. For the most part, schools have taken the place of apprenticeships as a place to teach these skills. There are about 50 public and private schools in America that offer some type of training in horse-shoeing, which vary a great deal in length and content. A good farrier school should emphasize mastery of the basics and provide a planned experience that allows you enough time to develop your skills and help you compete. The facilities should be safe and clean, and there should be a low student-teacher ratio. Good equipment should be available for study and practice after hours. The course should give you hands-on experience practicing how to handle the tools and how to work with horses, as well as extensive practical experience in anatomy, physiology, pathology, conformation (shape), and biomechanics of the horse.

The most successful farriers really understand the horse's foot, how to run a business, and have excellent horse and people communication skills. Metal forging technological skills are also vital.

Any school should be considered as only an introduction and a beginning to learning the horseshoeing trade. Because the condition of a horse's hoof is so important to the horse's health, the best farriers are those who have been trained in formal horseshoeing programs or have apprenticed under a master farrier. Those who go through additional training usually receive the best rates, and also can be confident that they're doing the best possible job.

Most farriers work for themselves, and spend most of their time traveling to farms and stables for scheduled shoeing appointments. In some cases, they may work at racetracks. The largest professional stables and horse farms will sometimes have a permanent farrier on staff.

Pitfalls

Shoeing horses is physically, mentally, and emotionally challenging, and it's potentially dangerous—you're picking up a horse's hoof shod in heavy metal, with your head in close proximity. You're in a vulnerable position beside an animal weighing hundreds of pounds. Painful kicks and bites are commonplace. Because of the physical demands of this job, you may only have a few good years to generate income—and when you can't work, you don't earn. Also, it takes time and training, close supervision, and a lot of practice to become a skilled farrier. You need a certain amount of up-front money to buy the tools, equipment, and inventory of shoes and supplies to go into business. Farriers also spend a lot of time traveling around to their clients, who may be scattered across the countryside. Weekend and after-hours work is often necessary.

Perks

If you love horses and you enjoy working with them, becoming a farrier could be a terrific career. Horseshoeing has great income potential, and highly skilled farriers with sound business practices in an area with lots of horses can make an excellent income.

Get a Jump on the Job

The more experience you can get with horses, the better. Take riding lessons and volunteer at a local stable or equine clinic. Search the Web to find a farrier in your region and see if you can volunteer to work with him or her. If not, at least hang around the local stable when the farrier comes to shoe the horses, and watch exactly what transpires. Read everything you can about horsemanship and a farrier career.

GOURMET DOG TREAT BAKER

OVERVIEW

Americans have more money and more time to lavish on their pets than ever before—and as we become more concerned with nutrition and diet, it's no surprise that we're also worried about keeping our dogs and cats fit and happy as well. In fact, the fastest growing segment of the pet foods industry is gourmet dog treats. Commercial dog biscuits are often filled with additives and chemicals, and home-baked goodies for Fido can eliminate all that unnecessary stuff.

There's a lot of money to be made in the gourmet pet treat biz, with its very high profit margin and eager markets of people with disposable incomes willing to purchase the best dog treats money can buy. And that means a ready market for natural, organic, or carefully homemade food and biscuits for dogs, despite the fact that all-natural handmade biscuits cost up to 10 times more than commercially-produced biscuits.

Sound like a good career to you? Making dog biscuits at home is easy, because all you need to get started are a few tasty dog biscuit recipes, healthy ingredients, biscuit molds (specially shaped molds such as bones, cars, or cats are big hits), a catchy name, packaging materials, and a good marketing plan.

You can start your company off right in your own home, using ingredients from your local grocery store to produce dog treats in your own oven, using parsley, eggs, milk, garlic, cheddar cheese, bone meal, pumpkin seeds, unsulfured molasses, car-

rots, celery, and oatmeal. You can choose a variety of flours for your treats, and because some dogs are allergic to wheat, think about offering a few non-wheat choices as well, such as rice, oat, or soy flour.

Producing food at home means lower production costs and a healthier bottom line. Unlike producing food for humans, which requires all kinds of state and federal safety guidelines and professional kitchens, the government is not nearly so picky about whipping up pet food in your own kitchen. Your area may require you to buy a basic business license if you produce the biscuits in your home, but that's about all. Some cities require "home occupation permits" or similar special licenses for home-based businesses.

Once your goodies are baked, you'll need to package them in a variety of interesting ways. You might offer the treats in a brown paper bag with a fancy bow, shrink-wrapped biscuit-filled tins, dog bowls, or

Daryl Ostrovsky, dog biscuit chef

Daryl Ostrovsky is that rarity in the pet food business—an award-winning chef who got into the dog biscuit business from a technical cooking background, rather than being a pet owner who loves pooches.

He started out, as many kids do, with dreams of becoming a vet. When the reality of the type of schooling he'd need to complete hit home, he changed course, and veered off into the food business—the human food business.

The idea to start a dog bakery really began when Ostrovsky was living in Atlanta with his one-year-old dog Cosmo, attending the School of Culinary Arts. "Going to chef's school, I became fascinated with reading labels, understanding all the types of ingredients that were in foods," he recalls. "In looking for treats for Cosmo, I noticed that there were more and more companies in this type of business. As good as some of these treats were, I knew I could make something that tasted better and was substantially healthier."

After graduating from culinary school, he started working as chef at various Atlanta restaurants, including a stint as a pastry chef. He finally decided to take the dog food plunge after he realized that running a restaurant was a lot of work with not much reward. "I was working crazy hours, and not having any fun," he says.

After he tested a few recipes, his first finished recipe was the peanut butter biscuit (a canine favorite), now called "Cosmo's Biscuits." He soon expanded the line to include chicken, ginger, and mint biscuits.

Then came an opportunity to open a bakery and small retail store just for dogs in Portland; Cosmo and Ostrovsky moved there, and the Great Dog Bakery opened its doors in March 2001. "The best part of this job is that my dog gets to work with me," he says. "He didn't do well when he was left by himself." Ostrovsky also loves watching his canine customers enjoy his biscuits.

There are a lot of homemade dog food biscuit chefs out there, but Ostrovsky suspects he's one of the very few professionally trained as a chef. He makes sure he uses only the finest and freshest quality ingredients, free of preservatives and artificial additives, and his biscuits are baked fresh to order.

"My great dog Cosmo is my resident taste-tester and I offer nothing to my customers that hasn't gotten his personal stamp of approval," he says. "I'm not knocking the other companies, but nobody uses the ingredients I use. I won't buy frozen chicken. I buy fresh skinless boneless chicken breasts and remove all the fat. Then I freeze the chicken and use it in my biscuits."

The Great Dog Bakery sells its biscuits online, at dog shows, and is currently negotiating to move its products to Amsterdam. "I'm happy to sell my dog biscuits anywhere it's legal to do so," he says. With the launching of his Web site, his treats are now available to dog lovers everywhere. "I'm living my dream of doing something with and for dogs," he says.

baskets. You'll also want to invest in labels or stickers for each of your products that list all ingredients, to ensure that your customers know exactly what they're getting.

Then it's time to market what you've made. To start off, research your community to identify places where you'll be able to sell your products—such as independent and chain pet retailers on a wholesale basis, or to consumers via pet fairs, dog shows, or directly from your home. Vet offices may be willing to carry your products, as may upscale pet stores, pet product stores, kennels, and even gift stores. If dogs truly love your treats, word-of-mouth advertising will be easy. You also can set up a Web site and sell through the mail, or create a catchy mail order catalog. Some biscuit producers limit their wares to wholesale, while others scout out a storefront and sell their product themselves. (This requires quite a bit of an investment, not to mention business savvy.)

Pitfalls

You've got to have a head for business in this job, and you'll have to make sure it's legal to prepare and sell dog food from your home (laws will vary from area to area).

Once you become successful, you reach that difficult stage where you must decide what to do yourself and what duties to delegate. Most specialty pet food chefs don't have formal cooking training, although the few who do have that much more chance of success.

Perks

If you love dogs, you love cooking and you dream of running your own business, what could be a better way to spend your talents? Dog biscuit chefs who also have a storefront have the added fun of actually seeing dogs enjoying their biscuits. And because the specialty pet food market is booming, there are more and more opportunities to design your own pet treats and set up your own business, either from a storefront or via mail order.

Get a Jump on the Job

If you love dogs and you love to cook, you can start now by reading as much as you can about healthy foods for dogs. Try getting a job at a kennel or your vet to learn as much as you can about canine nutrition. Also try learning as much as you can about cooking and running a business.

HOLISTIC VETERINARIAN

OVERVIEW

Barbara Vaughan's purebred kitten had been miserable with a stubborn viral infection for almost a year, with running eyes and stuffy nose that sometimes got so severe it struggled to breathe. Two different New Hampshire traditional vets were unable to cure the infection, and advised her that, with luck, the kitten would simply outgrow the problem. But a referral to a holistic vet changed everything, Vaughan says. Prescribing various homeopathic remedies designed to boost the kitten's immune system, within one week of treatment the kitten's eyes cleared, and the stuffy nose went back to normal. For the first time in its life, the kitten could breathe normally.

Rather than miracle cures, holistic vets—who are trained as traditional veterinarians—take a different approach to animal illness, turning to herbs, vitamins, minerals, flower essences, homeopathic remedies, and chiropractic or acupuncture to treat their patients. Holistic vets are highly educated veterinary professionals, but they've also gone through additional training in other branches of natural healing as well. Holistic veterinary medicine (also called integrative veterinary medicine) is a way of diagnosing an animal that takes into consideration the animal's entire life, combining conventional and alternative (or complementary) treatments.

There are basic differences between holistic and traditional veterinary medicine. Traditional veterinary medicine tends to divide the animal into a physical set of

(continues)

AT A GLANCE (continued)

states also do other testing on clinical competency. There are few reciprocal agreements between states, so it's not easy for a vet to practice in a different state without first taking another state examination. Most states have continuing education requirements for licensed veterinarians, which may involve attending a class or otherwise demonstrating knowledge of recent medical and veterinary advances.

Outlook

Employment opportunities are expected to be very good, although competition for admission to veterinary school is keen. The number of graduates from veterinary school is not expected to increase significantly over the 2002–12 period. As pets are increasingly viewed as a member of the family, and as pet owners are more and more interested in holistic methods for both humans and pets, they will be more willing to spend increasing amounts on advanced holistic veterinary medical care, creating more demand for holistic veterinarians. Also, more pet owners are buying pet insurance, increasing the likelihood that a considerable amount of money will be spent on veterinary care for their pets.

The techniques used in holistic medicine are gentle, minimally invasive, and emphasize the pet's well-being, focusing on the animal's "big picture" (including symptoms, the pet's environment, and the relationship of pet and owner). According to the National Holistic Veterinary Medical Association, holistic thinking is centered on love, empathy, and respect.

During an appointment, the holistic vet first does a comprehensive physical exam and asks the owner about the pet's behavior, medical history, diet, and any emotional or other stress, as well as the pet's genetics, nutrition, and hygiene. These questions and observations help the holistic vet uncover the true source of the pet's problem.

In many situations, treatment may combine standard western-style surgery and drug treatments along with alternative methods. Almost every type of human holistic medicine therapy also can be used with animals. Holistic vets may prescribe nutritional therapy using a specific preservative-free, environmentally sound diet. Holistic vets also may prescribe meganutrients (also known as orthomolecular medicine), including minerals, vitamins, and nutrients to correct deficiencies, prevent disease, and heal damaged tissue.

Many holistic vets are experts in acupuncture and traditional Chinese medicine, which they use to strengthen the animal's immune system, relieve pain, and improve the function of organs by stimulating acupuncture points on the body. In addition, many holistic vets also use homeopathic remedies or Bach flower essences, which are made from plants, minerals, and herbs (including North American herbs, Ayurvedic herbs from India, traditional Chinese herbs, and others). Some holistic vets also use chiropractic, which can be used to treat a broad spectrum of conditions in

organs, muscles, joints, and tissue systems, and treat each isolated area. A traditional vet looks at symptoms, assigns a disease or syndrome, and treats the animal with surgery, drugs, chemicals, or radiation. Holistic vets, on the other hand, treat each part of the animal as a part of the whole (which is where the name *holistic* comes from). Holistic vets believe that you can't cure the physical body by focusing on symptoms alone. Holistic medicine treats the body, the mind, and the spirit together, recognizing that these areas are interdependent. Traditional veterinary medicine concentrates mostly on the body.

Dr. Katherine Evans, holistic veterinarian

Frustration at not being able to ease chronic pain in arthritic dogs led Dr. Katherine Evans on a long journey into holistic veterinary medicine to find the answers unavailable in traditional methods. Her discovery that acupuncture can truly ease pain in dogs introduced her to an entirely new career path.

After graduating in 1992 from the University of Florida, College of Veterinary Medicine, Dr. Evans had started working as a traditional vet at a small animal clinic in Arlington, Virginia. "After about six months into my first job, I had a client with a dog who had arthritis," she says. "When I told her there was nothing else we could do—well, that wasn't an option for her. So I thought, what else is there for chronic pain in some of these animals?"

Not having an answer prompted Dr. Evans to search for the solution elsewhere. "I pursued my acupuncture training, hoping to provide an answer for that client and many other patients not well served by pharmaceutical drugs or surgery."

During that time, she adopted a black lab puppy with severe hip and elbow dysplasia. Alpha had had surgery on both her hips and her elbows, but remained inactive because of the pain. After just one acupuncture treatment, she was suddenly able to jump on the bed for the first time. "I was at once both awestruck and convinced that acupuncture worked," Dr. Evans says.

In 1994, she completed her acupuncture training under the auspices of the International Veterinary Acupuncture Society (IVAS). More and more clients began to flock to her with questions, and her interest in holistic and complementary veterinary medicine expanded. "It was more from the perspective of what clients asked me to help them with," she says, "and my feeling that there had got to be something that can be done." She began to study Chinese herbs as well.

In search of a slower pace, she moved to New Hampshire, and by 1998 she was ready to venture out on her own: the Holistic Veterinary Center, a referral-based vet facility offering a wide range of alternative and complementary therapies for dogs and cats including acupuncture, herbal medicine, chiropractic care, homeopathy, nutritional consultations, and wellness care. It's a practice that thrives on word of mouth. "People who come to see me are usually self referred," she says. "Most had a friend or coworker who heard about it. I just have a wonderful mix of people who truly want to do this stuff for their animals.

"It has progressed to where I am today," she says. "I do some traditional medicine. We do have people bring new puppies and kittens to see us, but who want to approach things from a different angle." Dr. Evans calls herself a "minimalist" when it comes to vaccinations. "I try to keep things simple, focus on diet and wellness when the pet is young," she says. Dr. Evans also does routine surgery, spays, and neuters. Anything requiring hospitalization or extensive testing is sent to the client's primary vet.

Just as with humans, holistic medicine for animals isn't always well accepted by older vets and older clients. "There's still a subset of people who are against it," she says. "An older population who doesn't really understand what it's about, but more are learning to accept it. Quite a few vets have brought their pets to me, and I have lots of vet support staff who come."

If learning to be a holistic vet seems to be in your future, you'll still have to carve out your own specialty, however. All holistic vets must first be licensed traditional vets who have graduated

(continues)

(continued)

from veterinary school, most of which only offer a course or two in holistic medicine. About eight programs across the country offer a student association for holistic medicine, Dr. Evans says, who get together and offer lectures.

If this sounds like something you'd enjoy, you need to work on getting good grades so you can make it to vet school. "Beyond that, there are a lot of lectures given by health food stores on different theories of aspects of holistic and natural medicine," Dr. Evans says. "The more you know, the easier it is." It's also possible to go through a human acupuncture or herbal medicine course, she says. Most of the acupuncture points used on dogs and cats were originally developed for people, she explains, and so they are thought to be similar. "But the more acupuncture done on dogs and cats, the more we realized some points don't have the same actions as in people.

"There are still a minority of schools that offer holistic programs, although Tufts and Colorado State have acupuncture courses," she says. Today, veterinary students spend a lot more time doing externship rotations during the junior and senior years, and those can be molded to whatever the individual wants. "If you have a holistic perspective, quite a few practitioners have students who come in and spend two or three weeks learning this aspect of veterinary medicine."

Once you graduate, she explains, you can pursue your own acupuncture program, Chinese herbal program, or a chiropractic certification program. All are overseen by the IVAS.

The joy of holistic veterinary medicine lies in giving people hope, Dr. Evans believes. "When they come to see me, it's usually because the people have run out of options. I like giving them potentially some options. Usually we can give them something we can try. I like being able to help both the pet and the owner feel better."

animals, since it is effective for any patient with a spine, bones, joints, and muscles.

Most holistic veterinarians perform clinical work in private practices, and more than half specialize in small companion animals such as dogs, cats, birds, reptiles, and rabbits. Another 25 percent work in mixed animal practices, which includes pigs, goats, sheep, and some non-domestic animals. Holistic veterinarians diagnose animal health problems, treat animals suffering from infections or illnesses, dress wounds, set fractures, perform surgery, and advise owners about animal feeding, behavior, and breeding. Many holistic vets, however, are opposed to extensive vaccinations that are normally performed by traditional vets.

Pitfalls

Solo practitioners often work extended and weekend hours, responding to emergencies or squeezing in unexpected appointments. When working with animals that are frightened or in pain, holistic veterinarians risk being bitten, kicked, or scratched. There is also a substantial financial investment required to purchase equipment, office space, and staff in order to set up an independently owned practice or purchase an established one. Moreover, it's not easy becoming a holistic vet—there's keen competition for admission to veterinary school (only one in three applicants was accepted in 2002). Private clinical practice is especially stressful because you need to invest in equipment and medicines.

Perks

If you love animals and sincerely want to help them, it can be incredibly rewarding to spend your time all day helping pets feel better. Holistic vets are normally dedicated to more natural types of medicine and enjoy using their skills in this way.

Get a Jump on the Job

While you're still in high school, you can volunteer at a holistic vet's office or a local pet store, kennel, stable, zoo, wildlife rehabilitation center, or animal shelter to learn more about working with animals. Take some courses in natural healing, and read all you can about homeopathy, acupuncture, therapeutic animal massage, chiropractic medicine, herbs and vitamins, and Bach flower essences.

In college, declare a pre-vet major, which emphasizes the sciences. Veterinary medical colleges typically require classes in organic and inorganic chemistry, physics, biochemistry, general biology, animal biology, animal nutrition, genetics, vertebrate embryology, cellular biology, microbiology, zoology, and systemic physiology. Some programs require calculus; some require only statistics, college algebra and trigo-nometry, or precalculus. Most veterinary medical colleges also require core courses, including some in English or literature, the social sciences, and the humanities. Increasingly, courses in practice management and career development are becoming a standard part of the curriculum to provide a foundation of general business knowledge for new graduates.

In addition to satisfying preveterinary course requirements, applicants also must submit test scores from the Graduate Record Examination (GRE), the Veterinary College Admission Test (VCAT), or the Medical College Admission Test (MCAT), depending on the preference of each college. Currently, 22 schools require the GRE, 4 require the VCAT, and 2 accept the MCAT.

Some vet schools rely a lot on your veterinary and animal experience in admittance decisions. Formal experience, such as work with veterinarians or scientists in clinics, agribusiness, research, or some area of health science, is particularly good. Less formal experience, such as working with animals on a farm, ranch, stable, or animal shelter, is helpful. The schools want to see a student display ambition and an eagerness to work with animals.

HORSE WHISPERER

OVERVIEW

The audience is silent, spellbound, as they watch the lone human in the center of the ring—using only voice and body—turn a wild, frightened, potentially deadly animal into an adoring trusting pet. It often takes a horse whisperer just a few minutes to enact this startling transformation.

Horse whispering involves a way of communicating with horses in such a way as to instill a sense of safety, peace, and confidence in the horse. With proper guidance, these special trainers say that anyone can learn more about the nature of horses, their language, and the communication skills required to have successful relations with them, including overcoming fear.

A horse whisperer is a special kind of equine trainer, who works with "difficult" horses using a very special, gentle type of training that emphasizes an understanding of the animal's basic instincts and fears. There is no place for fear or punishment in a horse whisperer's world.

These gifted trainers are self-employed, traveling the country to work with individual horse owners to overcome problems with the horse and rider. Hours are typically long and the work can be challenging as a horse whisperer exercises horses, accustoms them to reins and harnesses, and overcomes behavioral problems. The whisperer typically plans, supervises, and carries out special training programs for problem horses. Much of the work also involves marketing, publicizing the trainer's unique methods and philosophy.

Some master whisperers teach other trainers their unique methods. While different horse whisperers may use slightly different techniques (some, for example, insist on using a round pen; others say that a round pen is not necessary)— all of these trainers specialize in gentle understanding of a horse's natural inclination.

Winning a horse's trust is more important than breaking his spirit, according to the

---

AT A GLANCE

Salary Range

As a self-employed expert, horse whisperers' salaries vary widely depending on how aggressively they market their services, and whether they also offer books, CDs and DVDs, tapes, performances, and teaching. Depending on these services, income may range from $50,000 to well beyond $150,000 a year for a seasoned pro.

Education/Experience

Although there is no required type of formal education, horse whisperers are only as good as their reputation and experience. Most have spent a lifetime with horses and are extremely experienced horsemen and women, and have developed their own system of natural training.

Personal Attributes

Horse whisperers must have excellent communication skills with humans and horses; other skills include gentleness, compassion, honesty, kindness, empathy, "horse sense," and the ability to market themselves and their special type of training.

Requirements

Whisperers must have years of experience working with and training horses.

Outlook

Fair. The success of a horse whisperer is due in part because there aren't many who have this unique combination of gentle training and rapport with horses that enable the person to take a wild, uncontrollable animal and turn it into a gentle, well-trained horse.

Frank Bell, horse whisperer

Frank Bell lost his mother at the age of six, and turned to his best friend—a cocker spaniel—for comfort. Soon he became an expert at reading his dog's moods, and then he began reaching out to other dogs. "By age 10 I was ruining junkyard dogs by befriending them," he says. "It became a personal challenge to take on the meanest snarling dogs I could find. I simply wouldn't leave until I had the dogs licking my hand." Even as he worked with dogs, as a child he dreamed of owning his own horse and riding his best friend into the wilderness.

That's where it all started. It has taken Frank Bell about 20 years to work out his theories of training horses. "When I come from the perspective of genuine caring for the animal, and the horse understands that, we accomplish amazing things," he explains. "The symmetry of two living creatures interacting so each becomes a whole, is truly magical."

Bell seeks out the most difficult and dangerous horses to work with. Without using any type of force or cruelty, Bell transforms the horse's distrust of humans and the horse's problems into accomplishments. Soon the horse is giving to Bell exactly what is wanted, and doing so out of a willingness to please. "The word 'love' would not be inappropriate here," he says.

When making first contact with a horse, Bell tries very hard to make a lasting, unforgettable good first impression. With careful moves, he explores the animal using a gentle type of touching, which horses typically enjoy. As the horse's tension fades away, the bonding begins. Through gentle touch, Bell communicates trust and love, and spends all his time reinforcing these feelings. Once this communion is established, horses will do amazing things for Bell. Horses that seemed totally out of control only minutes before will suddenly become putty in his hands.

He focuses on developing a safe relationship with each horse, so that proper training lowers the tendency for the horse's instinct to explode and flee. When a horse is properly trained, Bell explains, the incidence of dangerous instinctive behavior fades away. A sudden surprise to the horse will trigger only a moderate, short-term reaction. "When trust is properly developed, the horse can tolerate almost anything," Bell says. "And the horse would do almost anything before it would endanger the rider."

Once a bond of trust has been established, Bell asks for a simple response from the horse, and then rewards the horse with praise when it delivers. Soon he can have "unmanageable" horses performing willingly and with enthusiasm.

Because each horse has unique problems, Bell figures out what is bothering the horse and addresses that specific issue.

Many horse owners simply avoid problem areas, Bell explains. One owner might insist his horse refuses to be cross-tied in an aisle; another says his horse won't jump in a ring. These behavior problems that the owner avoids are the first place he looks for. "Find the problem and fix it," he says. "Only then can the horse develop to its potential."

Bell has developed what he calls a 7-Step Safety System to take most of the risk out of riding by dealing with problems before ever mounting a horse. With this type of solid foundation, the horse becomes more confident and safer to ride. His 7-Step Safety System begins with bonding between man and horse. "Taking the time to love on the horse pays big rewards only minutes later as the horse eagerly chooses to give back and enjoy performing and engaging with the human," Bell says. "It is truly magical."

(continues)

(continued)

The first step is to quickly find that secret place that can melt a horse, Bell says. "If I can find that, then I'm light years ahead." The horse's eyes are his favorite "melting zone," followed by the mouth and tongue, the ears, the "V" under the jaw, and the withers (the highest part of the back at the base of the neck). "The trick is to find it quickly and indulge the horse momentarily." Then, the moment the horse starts to relax, Bell stops and walks away, which leaves the horse begging for more. "I typically walk away from that horse and within seconds that same horse is right there begging for more." Right away, Bell says, the horse is beginning to trust you. "I'm asked to work with aggressive, abused, man-hating animals all the time and in most cases I can turn them around in seconds by simply giving to them."

After locating a horse's specific fear, Bell breaks that fear down to the smallest step and figures out how to get the horse over the problem, exposing the horse to what it's afraid of in an unthreatening way while constantly touching. He tries to keep things interesting and returns to the bonding method whenever necessary, explaining that when the horse shows fear, you need to back off, going back to gently touch the eyes, the corner of the mouth, feathering the tongue, and touching under the jaw. You want to get the horse to drop the head.

"My dream is to share this philosophy with mankind on every level," Bell says, "as horses and humans heal each other and ultimately realize their full potential."

horse whisperer, and getting the trust is as simple as figuring out the animal's basic fear and getting him to trust you to overcome it.

Pitfalls

Horse whisperers may need to work long hours, and extensive travel is often involved. Much of their work is carried out very early in the morning and they may continue to work all day, often under harsh conditions. There is also a certain amount of danger in working with large animals. In addition, many whisperers say it can be frustrating to deal with people and their misconceptions, misunderstanding, and unfounded opinions about horses, along with their egos.

Perks

A horse whisperer chooses this profession because he or she loves horses, understands them, and is able to maintain a unique bond with the horse. It can be enormously satisfy-ing to start with a frightened, angry, difficult horse and end up with a calm, happy animal who can work well with its owner. Turning fear into trust in any human or animal is a special endeavor. Very successful horse whisperers may become quite famous, and offer books, tapes, videos, and travel the world teaching their training methods. For these whisperers, there is a certain amount of fame and a healthy salary.

Get a Jump on the Job

Work with horses just as soon as you can, and spend as much time as possible simply observing their behavior. Volunteer at a local stable or therapeutic riding center, join a 4-H pony club, and take riding lessons if you can. Read widely about all kinds of horses and training methods and watch trainers working with horses whenever possible. Some colleges offer equine science courses and majors.

MARINE MAMMAL TRAINER

OVERVIEW

Who wouldn't want to throw a fish to Flipper, swim with dolphins, and get to work with fascinating marine mammals? These creatures seem to capture the attention and imagination of just about everyone, and many people dream of becoming whale or dolphin trainers. Anyone who has ever seen a whale or dolphin show can appreciate the talents of both the trainers and the animals.

A marine mammal trainer (also called animal care specialists, keepers, naturalists, or mammalogists) uses information from marine biology and oceanography to train dolphins, whales, seals, sea lions, walruses, and other marine mammals using positive reinforcement.

The four orders of marine mammals include whales, dolphins, porpoises, seals, sea lions, walruses, dugongs, manatees, sea otters, and polar bears. Of these, trainers most often work with whales, dolphins, seals, and sea lions, spending a lot of time making the animals feel comfortable and helping them get acclimated to their surroundings. Marine mammals require specific aquatic environments, and because they are social creatures that cannot thrive without social opportunities, they need well designed and maintained living spaces, physical and mental stimulation, and proper medical care.

Training can be an extremely important way to help meet these goals, as well as teaching behaviors to the mammals. But

AT A GLANCE

Salary Range

Animal trainers in general aren't highly paid, and marine mammal trainers are no exception. You can expect to earn anywhere from $6 to $9 an hour to start. Facilities located in areas where the cost of living is very high may pay up to $12 an hour for a starting trainer, but that is the exception. A senior trainer with 8 to 12 years experience can expect to earn between $25,000 and $40,000 a year, depending on the location and individual facility.

Education/Experience

There are no established educational requirements for marine mammal trainers, but most employers require trainers to have at least a bachelor's degree in a field such as biology, zoology, or animal behavior. Some employers will hire trainers who have completed a two-year program in training exotic animals. However, there has been a continuing trend in the industry toward increased demand for greater education and advanced degrees.

Personal Attributes

You must be able to relate well to animals. You should have hands-on experience in some type of animal husbandry. Good communication skills are essential, since you'll be dealing with both animals and people. Training marine animals is very physical work, so you'll do much better if you're in good physical condition.

Requirements

Most facilities require their training staff to be certified scuba divers. You also need to be fit, able to swim well, have excellent showmanship ability, and be able to assist with cleaning equipment, helping to maintain filtration systems, and other jobs. Other requirements vary depending on the employer, but often include excellent public speaking skills.

Outlook

Marine mammal facilities are few and far between, and training marine mammals appeals to a great many people. As a result, there are many more applicants for jobs than jobs. Job growth in this field is expected to be slower than average.

this job entails much more than spending a few hours tossing fish into the pool. Animal trainers also prepare food for their charges, fill out food and behavior records, unload fish delivery trucks (a marine mammal facility goes through an amazing amount of fish every day), attend meetings, supervise apprentice trainers, keep the facility clean, and participate in public education.

Animal trainers are expected to have a fair amount of veterinary knowledge, and must be able to recognize quickly if their animals seem to be ill or not acting like themselves. This can be difficult, because marine mammals can become quite sick without exhibiting any symptoms. That means marine mammal trainers need to be able to interpret animal signs and body language, and sense when a problem is occurring.

Trainers work with whales and dolphins using the tools of psychology and behavior analysis based on positive reinforcement, a technique that rewards the animals for their correct responses with food and touching. Trainers develop plans for each animal, what cues and reinforcers they'll use, and then they work with each animal to achieve the desired behaviors. A trainer working with a marine mammal teaches dozens of behaviors during each training session. How long it takes to teach a behavior depends on its complexity, the animal-trainer relationship, and the physical condition and motivation of the animal.

During a typical day as a trainer at a marine mammal facility, you'll start by punching in and checking on your assigned animals. When you're sure that all is well and the animals are healthy, it's time to fix their breakfast. This involves sorting, checking, rinsing, and weighing fish, cleaning up the food preparation area, and stor-

ing unused fish in the refrigerator. Then it's time to feed your mammals with the fish and any vitamins prescribed by a veterinarian, and record each animal's food intake and behavior. After breakfast it's time to clean the animals' living spaces. Training, performances, and demonstrations occur throughout the day, and you'll also need to make time to simply be with the animals, getting to know each one and earning its trust and companionship. You'll need to maintain your area of the facility and perform any repairs, as necessary. You might help with a veterinary procedure, work with interns or apprentice trainers, attend a meeting, or read about what's happening within the industry.

Before you leave for the day, you'll need to clean the animals' living area again, feed your animals, and remove fish from the freezer for the next day's breakfast. You'll fill out the day's final records, and you'll need to make sure that all areas have been secured. After one last check on the animals, you'll shower and change into clean clothes, punch out at the time clock, and head home. If it's your turn to be on call, however, there's no guarantee that you won't be back at the facility long before the next morning to assist with a birth, a health problem, or other sort of emergency.

Pitfalls

The biggest downfall to a career in marine mammal training is that there are so few jobs. Also, because most marine mammal facilities are run as nonprofit agencies and there are more people looking for jobs than there are jobs, the pay for trainers is relatively low. If you do get a job, you'll find that it's very time consuming, because the animals require care 24 hours a day, seven days a week. The job entails work-

Terry S. Samansky, marine mammal trainer

Terry S. Samansky has worked with marine mammals for more than 20 years, and has enjoyed every minute of it.

"You have to be really dedicated to the business," he says, "and you have to really love the animals." He's had hands-on experience with dolphins, whales, seals, sea lions, and walruses, working as a trainer, care specialist, and facility curator, director, and consultant. He is a former director of marine mammals for Marine World in Vallejo, California, just north of San Francisco, where he trained dolphins and killer whales.

Samansky, who has a bachelor's degree in vertebrae biology with a minor in chemistry, says the extremely competitive nature of this job field is making it increasingly necessary to have a college degree before entering. Even more important than the education, however, he says, is getting all the experience you can. This can include internships, volunteer jobs, and training under an experienced trainer.

Although most job descriptions for marine mammal trainers outline eight-hour work days, Samansky says a typical day often is much longer, featuring 60- and even 80-hour work weeks during the busiest seasons, or when there are births, health problems with animals, long-distance transports, or extreme weather situations.

ing on weekends and holidays (animals must be fed 365 days a year), which can make planning for social events difficult.

Perks

It is extremely rewarding to establish and nurture a relationship with a marine mammal that grows to trust you and try to please you. In addition, trainers tend to forge close bonds with one another, making for a pleasant working environment. You also get to educate the public about the uniqueness and importance of marine mammals.

Get a Jump on the Job

Get some experience around animals in whatever way you can. Volunteer at a local zoo, veterinary office or hospital, aquarium, animal shelter, or horse stable—wherever animals are to be found. Once you're in college, look for internship positions—these are extremely important. Read all that you can about training animals, particularly marine mammals. Take all the psychology and related courses you can, and talk to other people who work with animals.

MUSHER

OVERVIEW

Through mounds of snow and ice, biting wind and howling storms, the musher guides the sled through the frozen wilderness. Dog mushers—also known as sled-dog tour guides—train dogs to pull sleds over snow and ice. Some mushers compete in grueling races, such as the Iditarod Trail Sled Dog Race, held each year in Alaska. Others offer sled-dog tours to tourists and visitors who are willing to pay for the adventure.

It's a tough, independent life in the far north, because mushing is hard work; you've got to be in excellent physical condition to be able to handle dogs effectively and safely. In fact, most employers require mushers to be able to meet minimum physical fitness requirements, and others expect employees to embark on a vigorous training program before the sled-dog tour season begins to ensure they'll be in peak condition.

The basic job of mushing takes a fair degree of training as well. Mushers use various signals to guide teams of dogs harnessed to specially made sleds. It's important to know and understand each dog on the team and how each dog relates to the others. Just like people, not all dogs get along and can work well together.

If you get a job as a musher with a sled-dog tour company, you'll be expected to do much more than give rides to visitors. You'll also be required to help care for the dogs by feeding and watering them, cleaning their kennels, and attending to their health. If a dog gets loose or another problem occurs, you'll be expected to respond,

regardless of the time or weather. You also may be expected to help with chores, such as cutting and stacking firewood, mending harnesses, repairing sleds, and keeping the trails in order.

Because there's the possibility of accidents, a musher must be trained in first aid and safety. He or she will be

Wally and Denise Glass, mushers

Wally Glass and his wife, Denise, have run Mountain Mushers, Inc., a sled-dog tour business in Vail, Colorado, for 17 years. For them and their two children, the business is not just a way to make a living, it's a way of life.

"Dogsled tours aren't something we do just to make money," Denise says. "Animals are our life and we could not imagine life without them. Our dogs are very friendly and petlike, because they know that we truly love them."

The children help with raising puppies and feeding the dogs, while Denise tends to the business aspects of the business, such as paying bills, keeping track of reservations, and answering phone calls and e-mails from people with questions about the tours.

Wally hires and trains the mushers who work for him, and works hard to keep himself in good physical condition.

"You have to be very strong and also athletic," Wally says. "I don't really prepare myself physically for the season, I just try to be healthy and keep myself in shape all year round. It is more of a physical challenge to run the dogs because the trail is mountainous terrain in high altitudes."

A typical day for Wally during the sled-dog tour season (the season lasts as long as the snow does) is long. He's out by 6 a.m. to help the mushers care for the dogs and get them loaded into trucks that will take them to the trail he uses, about 45 minutes from the kennel.

Once they're at the trail, they get the dogs out of the trucks and put on their harnesses. Sleds must be prepared for customers by loading them up with blankets and pillows.

Guests arrive in vans and are assigned sleds. Wally has five sleds and runs five teams of 12 dogs at a time, with himself as one of the mushers. Each tour covers six miles and lasts for two hours, including a break on the trail for hot cocoa and pumpkin bread that Denise makes each day.

After a lunch break, a second round of guests arrives for an afternoon tour. When that's completed, the dogs have to be unharnessed, loaded back into the truck, and driven back to the kennel, where they are fed and cared for.

"We are out for 12 hours a day," Wally says. "We leave in the dark and we get home in the dark. Many people think they want to get into dog sledding, but it's not an easy career. You have long days outside in the cold and snow."

While offering dogsled tours can be lucrative—especially if you're located near a major ski resort and let people know that you're there—it's not without problems. "You don't make any money during the months of the year that you're not running, and the dogs require things all year round," Wally says. "Equipment is expensive. With our growing population, it's becoming almost impossible to find a place that is rural enough to keep a dog kennel and find enough land to make a trail."

Moreover, running a dogsled tour business requires a lot of knowledge about sled dogs, and a great deal of patience. You have to be willing to get to know each dog, he says, because each one has his or her own personality. "We have been in business in Vail for 17 years, and it has been a struggle every year to make it happen," Denise says. "But we love this so much that it has been worth every headache."

expected to react calmly and handle any sort of situation that might come up on the trail.

Mushers who run sled dogs have a lot of fun, but the job also involves spending long hours outside in freezing temperatures—day after day. Depending on the size of the operation and how many employees there are, a musher might be expected to be outside for 12 hours a day, preparing for and guiding sled-dog tours.

Pitfalls

Sled-dog touring is seasonal, so many mushers have to seek other jobs in the off-season. If you own the sled-dog tour company and the dogs, you'll need to be able to make enough money to support the dogs in the off-season. If you're planning to start your own sled-dog tour company, you'll need to buy or lease land. Some landowners will lease "running rights" to mushers.

Perks

People are willing to pay substantial fees for the experience of riding on a dogsled, creating the potential to make some serious dollars. Many employers will provide lodging and food in addition to a salary for mushers. You'll get to be in great shape and spend lots of time outdoors.

Get a Jump on the Job

If you live in an area where there are sled-dog tour companies, ask if you can start by cleaning kennels or doing other chores there. Some communities have mushing clubs that teach young people to run dogs and sponsor races in which they can participate. Get all the experience you can, and spend as much time as possible around sled dogs. This will help you to get comfortable being around a lot of animals.

PET CEMETERY OWNER

OVERVIEW

When a family has to put a beloved pet to sleep, the question of what to do with the animal's body can be a troubling one. Unless the owner lives in the country, there may not be room in the backyard to bury the body. What's an owner to do?

More than 400 active pet cemeteries in the United States have the answer. Most pet cemeteries operate in conjunction with other pet-related businesses, such as boarding kennels, grooming salons, training centers, and veterinary hospitals. Some human cemeteries have set aside a portion of their ground for pet burials, but most pet cemeteries are family owned and specifically dedicated to the burial or cremation of pets. The oldest known pet cemetery was uncovered in Green County, Illinois, by archaeologist Stewart Schrever, who thinks the pets were buried about 6500 B.C. The oldest operating pet cemetery in the United States is the Hartsdale Pet Cemetery in New York. America's first pet burial ground, the Hartsdale Pet Cemetery was founded by veterinarian Samuel Johnson in 1896, who agreed to bury the dog of a woman who had no place to inter her pet. From then on, more and more pets found their way to Johnson's orchard for burial, until he finally set aside three acres just for this purpose. Today, more than a century later, Johnson's beautiful hillside orchard is the final resting place for almost 70,000 dogs, cats, birds, and rabbits—and one lion cub. Some of the world's most well-known individuals (everyone from Diana Ross and Mariah Carey to Robert Merrill and the

late singer Kate Smith) have buried their pets at the Hartsdale Pet Cemetery, and pet

Sharon Keillor, pet cemetery owner

Ever since she was a child, Sharon Keillor loved animals and made sure that each and every one of her pets, from goldfish to dogs, had a proper burial when it died. "Nothing ever just got pitched," she says. "So owning a pet cemetery is kind of a natural offshoot of that."

For the past 27 years, she and her husband Bill have been running Pet Rest Gardens in Flushing, Michigan, which they bought along with a kennel.

Pet Rest offers full service burials with an endowed care section, which includes pickup (from home or vet), body care, casket, ground-level memorial, and permanent care. Prices begin at $600 and go up, depending on the size of the pet and any additional services. The cemetery also offers an affordable "country burial" option adjacent to the regular cemetery, without headstones; caskets are possible but not required. Memorials for this section are placed on a "memorial board." The cemetery also offers memorial stones for home and cemetery burial.

In addition to burials, Keillor also offers cremation services—either a single cremation, or a group cremation in which other pets may also be cremated at the same time. Even in the group cremation, each pet is located separately in the unit, and owners are guaranteed that their own pet's ashes will be returned to them. Owners may choose to attend the cremation if they desire. Fees for cremation vary from $90 to $350 depending on the size of the pet, the type of cremation service, and includes the cost of an urn. Pet Rest provides free cremation for any certified guide dog, leader dog, rescue or K-9 dog, or service/tracking dogs.

Cremation actually makes up most of their pet cemetery business. "About 99 percent of people take the ashes home with them, rather than bury them," she explains. They have about 50 burials a year, but that has been declining steadily in favor of cremation—the same as for humans.

Keillor attributes the rise of cremation and the decline of burial to the tendency modern Americans have of moving from place to place, and the reluctance of pet owners to bury their pets (whether at home or in a cemetery)—risking leaving them behind when they move.

Although the job of burying or cremating pets may seem like a difficult or sad occupation, Keillor explains that as a pet lover, this really isn't the case. "I enjoy meeting great pets after their death," she says. "The majority of people who come here, I've never talked to or met prior to their pet dying. I've made great friends and met lots of wonderful people, and I've gotten to know posthumously some great pets."

She adds that while there's nothing she dislikes about the job, the unpredictable hours and constant availability needs some getting used to. "That saying that 'death never takes a holiday' is true," she says. "There are no standard hours or days off. Many times, I've gotten a call Christmas morning and had to go pick up a pet who's died at someone's house. It happens all the time."

If you're a pet lover and you're interested in owning a pet cemetery, Keillor cautions that loving animals isn't enough—you've also got to have a head for business. There are legal issues and business considerations to be aware of. "You should do your homework, and do your research into the business," she says. "There are those people—I call it the Bleeding Heart Syndrome. They think: 'I feel sorry for people who have no place to bury their pets.' But they need to realize that 10 years from now, it will still be a pet cemetery. You need to keep that in mind." She also advises that one of the best things you can do to prepare for this job is to work for a pet cemetery or do an apprenticeship to really understand what is entailed. "You must be compassionate, but you also must be a good business person.

"I love my job," she says, "and I wouldn't change it at all—well, except maybe to move it to a warmer climate!"

lovers from all walks of life have had pets buried and cremated at this cemetery.

The largest pet cemetery in the United States is Bide-A-Wee Home Association, also located in New York, which has more than 5,000 pets buried in one site alone. Bide-A-Wee operates at least three animal shelters, as well as its satellite pet cemeteries.

Still, only about 200 of the thousands of pets that die each day are ever buried in a pet cemetery. Some are interred in the owner's back yard, and others are cremated by veterinary hospitals. Local or county ordinances determine whether or not a pet can be buried at home.

Most pet cemetery owners also offer pet memorials, cremation services, headstones, and vaults. A standard pet plot may cost from $500 to $625 depending on location. Although basic markers may be included, fancier headstones (such as colored granite, or stones with a metal photo) would typically cost extra (from $45 to $65). Many cemeteries offer prepaid maintenance fees for five or ten years. Caskets are also typically offered for most pet sizes, and pet urns for cremated pets are usually offered by cemetery owners as well. Some cemetery owners offer a "memorial wall" with a pet's name inscribed, and simply scatter the pet's ashes at the site.

Typically, when a pet dies, either the owner or the vet calls the pet cemetery to make arrangements. Some cemeteries offer a "call service" to go pick up a pet that has died to remove for burial. If burial is chosen, the cemetery owner assigns an individual lot to the pet owner, and schedules the burial. Usually, the owner and family are allowed to view the pet in a casket and add any items belonging to the pet that they may wish to bury with the animal. The owners may or may not be present at the burial.

If the owners choose to cremate a pet, the animal is promptly cremated and the ashes given to the owner. If the owner doesn't want the ashes, some pet cemetery owners will scatter the ashes at a special site.

Many cemetery owners also offer a "pre-need" plan, in which owners make a down payment before a pet dies to reserve a grave of their choice, followed by monthly payments until the plan is paid for.

Pet cemetery owners must be aware of and follow all the legal technicalities that may apply to running a cemetery. They must be sure that the property is deeded to ensure pet owners that the animal's remains won't be disturbed by land development. The cemetery owner also should maintain a care fund (as do human cemeteries) to ensure that funds will be available to maintain the grounds and roads. Access should be kept open in the event of development around a pet cemetery, and the land should be owned by the proprietors or by a cemetery corporation. It should not be leased or rented.

Pitfalls

It can be emotionally wrenching to deal with bereaved pet owners who have lost a beloved animal, and being on call constantly can be stressful.

Perks

If you care about animals and you enjoy meeting with the public, this job can be personally fulfilling, as you help owners come to terms with personal loss.

Get a Jump on the Job

It may be possible to volunteer at a local pet cemetery to get an idea of how the business is run. In addition, any business skills you can pick up in high school or college will be quite helpful in starting a pet cemetery.

PET LAWYER

OVERVIEW

Your dog just bit the mailman. Or maybe you want to rent an apartment, and the lease says you can't have more than two cats. Perhaps you were upset at the condition of your dog after he gets off an airplane, or perhaps you've run afoul of leash laws, dog waste laws, occupancy laws, or rabies laws. A pet lawyer can provide the legal expertise to solve these and other pet problems.

Pet lawyers act as both advocates and advisors. As advocates, they represent the pet owner in criminal and civil trials by presenting evidence and arguing in court in support of their client. As advisors, lawyers counsel their clients about their legal rights and obligations and suggest particular courses of action in personal matters, such as how to provide for a pet's care after the owner's death. Whether acting as an advocate or an advisor, all attorneys research the intent of laws and judicial decisions and apply the law to the specific circumstances faced by their client.

Pet lawyers typically handle a wide variety of legal issues affecting pets, companion animals, and their people. The love that humans give their pets, and the circumstances in which they care for them, often leads to specific legal problems. A pet lawyer can defend a client from a prosecutor's dangerous dog charges, help clients understand their rights and obligations when buying or renting New York City apartments, and sue, defend, or appeal a jury's personal injury award in a dog bite lawsuit. Pet lawyers handle

AT A GLANCE (continued)

require the six-hour Multistate Bar Examination (MBE) as part of the general bar examination. (The MBE isn't required in Louisiana and Washington.) A local state bar exam may be given in addition to the MBE. In addition, a three-hour multistate essay examination (MEE) is part of the bar exam in several states.

Outlook

Excellent. Employment of lawyers is expected to grow about as fast as the average through 2012, primarily as a result of growth in the population. Demand for pet lawyers will be spurred by the growth of legal action in this area, which is a fairly new type of law. There are very few lawyers practicing this specialty, especially in the east. Pet lawyers who wish to work independently may want to establish a new practice in expanding suburban areas, where competition from larger, established law firms is likely to be less keen than in big cities, and new lawyers may find it easier to become known to potential clients.

custody battles, veterinary malpractice, wrongful death or injury, ownership disputes, sales and breeder contracts, and legal disputes involving pet care facilities, groomers, breeders, pet walkers/sitters, and more. Pet lawyers also help with pet disputes during divorces, support, and custody. They also handle estate planning to assure care of your pet.

When a landlord or cooperative apartment wants to evict a tenant because she has a dog or cat, the pet owner needs an attorney knowledgeable in landlord-tenant matters and legal defenses in pet-based eviction proceedings. Animal law encompasses many areas of practice, such as veterinary malpractice, animal bites, assurance of animal care after a pet owner's death, and custody disputes.

Animal law is not limited only to pets, however. It includes just about any kind of animal you can imagine, from companion animals to agricultural animals to exotic creatures normally found in zoos.

Pitfalls

Pet lawyers may work irregular hours while conducting research, conferring with clients, or preparing briefs. Lawyers often work long hours, and of those who regularly work full time, about half work 50 hours or more a week. They may face particularly heavy pressure at times, especially when a case is being tried.

Perks

Becoming a pet lawyer is one fairly new way to combine a law career with a love of animals, and activists who practice this type of law really love the idea that they are helping animals and their owners. There can be a lot of satisfaction in this type of work.

Get a Jump on the Job

Prospective pet lawyers should become skilled in writing and speaking, reading, researching, analyzing, and thinking logically—skills needed to succeed both in law school and in the profession. A multidisciplinary college background is recommended, with courses in English, foreign languages, public speaking, government, philosophy, history, economics, mathematics, and computer science, among others. Students interested in pet law may also find animal-related courses helpful.

Acceptance by most law schools depends on good undergraduate grades, the

Molly Maguire Gaussa, animal lawyer

As a law school grad, Molly Maguire Gaussa was distraught when she lost Jerry, her German shepherd mix, a victim of veterinary malpractice. "I had no idea I had any recourse," she says. "I missed him so much and it broke my heart. I decided I did not want anyone to go through what my parents and I went through with Jerry's loss." At first, she wasn't sure how she was going to help protect animals—but she knew she wanted to do something.

Armed with a new law degree, she realized she wanted to tie her love for animals into her new practice. "I'd opened my own office and after three short months I wanted to leave the legal profession," she says. As she was walking Casey Blue, her black lab, she wondered: "What can I do to tie my love for animals into my firm?" Gaussa remembered that her final paper in law school had focused on animal rights. "I began researching animal law to see if there is a need in Pennsylvania, and lo and behold—there was a need. I became one of the only known animal lawyers in the state."

Today, Gaussa is committed to the security and defense of rights for all people. In professional and personal life, Ms. Gaussa works hard for organizations that try to make life better for others—including the four-legged members of the population. Her animal cases include veterinary malpractice, animal bites, assurance of animal care after a pet owner's death, and custody disputes. "We desire to represent the party who has the best interest of the animal and the community at heart," she explains. She points out that animal law isn't limited to pets; it includes any animal, including farm animals.

Of course, the hard part about focusing on animal law is that often it exposes you to the seamier side of life. She finds it particularly hard to deal with what some animals must endure, such as abuse, vet malpractice, and defects from improper breeding.

Gaussa loves what she's doing, and she urges anyone who may be interested in becoming a lawyer to think about animal law. "The animals need us to help protect them," she says. "We are their voices. The animals need people to help them and protect them as living breathing beings."

The field is most popular in the West; from Ohio east, Gaussa says, it's hard to find a lawyer who specializes in animals. "I've had people contact me from Florida, New Jersey, Kansas, New York, and Ohio, all in search of an animal lawyer in their area."

Law School Admission Test (LSAT), the quality of the applicant's undergraduate school, any prior work experience, and sometimes a personal interview. All law schools approved by the ABA, except those in Puerto Rico, require applicants to take the LSAT.

PET PHOTOGRAPHER

OVERVIEW

Walk into almost any American living room and you'll see layers of photos decked out in silver, gold, or black frames, propped up on pianos, mantels, tables, and cabinets: bouncing babies, smiling grandmas, proud papas. These days, you'll also be likely to see snaps of the family pet, decked out in silly hats or pert bows, posing with the family.

While a decade or so ago there were very few photographers who specialized in taking pictures of pets, the number has increased dramatically as demand for their services has increased. Today, Americans spend more than $300 a year on their pets, including having Fido and Fifi photographed. And, as Americans are embracing more and more exotic animals as pets, pet photographers aren't only taking pictures of cats and dogs, but horses, snakes, fish, birds, lizards ferrets, and other animals, as well.

A pet photographer must have excellent general photography skills. He or she also, however, must have a thorough understanding of the particulars of taking photos of animals. Pet photographers must take into account the color and texture of the animal's fur or hair, the expression of the animals, how the ears are positioned, and if the animal seems to be tense or relaxed.

Some pet photographers prefer to have the pet's owner present as they are shooting, while others find that having the owners there is distracting to both the pet and the photographer.

AT A GLANCE

Salary Range

Photographers of all kinds, including pet photographers earn an average salary that ranges between $17,750 and $35,000, depending on the type of work, location, and other factors. Because pet photography is a niche market, a high-end photographer with a good clientele could expect to earn more. One high-profile pet photographer charges $850 for a 90-minute photo session.

Education/Experience

There are no specific educational requirements to become a pet photographer. Because a college degree can never hurt, ideally, you could take a four-year photography program at a college or university. Photography, however, also can be self-taught, learned as an apprentice, or learned at a technical school.

Personal Attributes

You should be creative, have good hand-eye coordination, and be able to work well with both pets and their owners. If you're in your own business, as many pet photographers are, you'll need to learn and develop business skills, as well as be an excellent photographer.

Requirements

A good knowledge of animals and understanding of the differences between different types and breeds of animals is essential. In addition, some municipalities require professional photographers to be licensed.

Outlook

Jobs for all photographers, including pet photographers, are expected to increase about as quickly as average through 2012.

Pet photographers will sometimes pose animals. You might find hamsters tucked into tea cups, or cats curled into cozy baskets, baby strollers, laundry baskets,

John Secoges, pet photographer

John Secoges has been asked to photograph horses, dogs, cats, birds, and snakes. His primary animal customers, however, are cats and dogs.

Secoges, who has been a professional photographer in Pennsylvania for many years, got into pet photography because he noticed there was a market for it. Families would ask to have their pets included in a family portrait. Or he'd be photographing a baby or child, and the parents would ask him about having their pet photographed.

The most difficult part of photographing animals, Secoges says, is getting them to cooperate. Just when you want a dog to sit down, he says, is when the dog will feel like getting up for a little walk.

Young, frisky dogs are particularly difficult, he says. When that scenario occurs, Secoges says he usually heads outside. "Older dogs usually are easier because they tend to be a little better disciplined," he says. "They'll just lie there and put up with it. If you get a wild puppy or young dog, though, I find it's best to go with it, and take action shots." Photographing a running dog, Secoges says, is rather like shooting a race car. You pan the camera on the moving animal, just as you would the speeding car.

Allowing the puppy to run around often has an additional benefit, Secoges says. "After awhile they get tired and lie down. Then you work with what you have and get a shot of the dog lying in a pile of leaves or on a nice patch of grass," Secoges says.

While education is very important, he says, hands-on experience is just as necessary. Secoges recalled that the very first roll of film he ever shot was of his pet cat.

"It was great experience, actually," he says. "I'd take pictures of her sitting in the window, and that would teach me about window light. I'd use a flash or not use a flash, and I could see what the differences were. I learned a lot from taking pictures of my own pets."

If you're just starting out in photography, you have even more advantages than photographers did in the past, due to the advent of digital cameras that allow you to see immediately what you've done right—or wrong. "That's a great learning curve," Secoges says. "You can see immediately where you did well or didn't do well. That's a big advantage. Students should take advantage of current technology, and keep up with whatever will be coming along."

buckets, swings, wagons, and hats. Some pet photographers photograph only pets, while others specialize in pets and their people. Some specialize in taking outdoor action shots of pets, while other photographers prefer studio shots.

If you're thinking about becoming a pet photographer, there are a number of ways you might consider setting up a business. You could offer pet photography in addition to other kinds of photos, or do pet photography exclusively.

Some pet photographers do only portrait-type shots, while others offer videotaping and action shots, as well. Some pet photographers are mobile, preferring to photograph the pet in its own environment, where it is most comfortable. Others specialize in photographing at pet shows. Some pet photographers offer a lot of extras, such as pet costumes, themed backdrops, cutesy frames, and transferring the pet's picture on t-shirts, key rings and so forth. Others are more straightforward and only deal in photographing the animals.

Regardless of what type of pet photography you offer, you need to realize that running a business requires business smarts. It's not enough to be a good photographer. You'll also have to consider issues such as setting rates, billing, marketing your services, scheduling and keeping track of appointments, and so forth.

Pitfalls

While Americans love their pets and spend tons of money on them, pet photography is subject to general economic conditions. Let's face it, food on the table and gas in the car will always take priority over a professionally done photograph of a pet. And, as pet photography becomes more commonly done and high profile, an increasing number of photographers are likely to jump into the field, possibly making for a competitive job field.

Perks

If you love animals, what could be more fun that earning money by photographing them? You get to meet new critters on a regular basis, and to create lasting memories for their owners.

Get a Jump on the Job

Get started by taking pictures of your own pets, your grandparents' pets, your cousin's pets, and your neighbor's pets. When you get some good shots, give them to the owners. Sign up for a photography course at a local arts school. Read everything that you can about photography and photographing animals. And work to expand your knowledge of animals and their behaviors. Most of all, though, practice, practice, and practice some more.

PET PSYCHIC

OVERVIEW

It's not spooky, or voodoo, or magic, pet psychics say, that enables them to connect with pets and help their owners understand them. Instead, they say it's a deep love of animals and a sensitivity to the thought processes of other creatures that helps them communicate in ways most of us cannot. Many insist that it's not a gift but is really a skill that any pet owner could develop, if they only practiced the ability to connect with their pets.

Pet psychics, also known as *animal communicators*, have one of the more unusual jobs in the animal world. Pet psychics are self-employed experts in understanding animal behavior on a deeper, more intuitive level. Most explain their ability to figure out what's going on in Fido's mind as the ability to receive "pictures" or sensations from the pet. Most pet psychics consult over the phone, speaking to the pet owner while telepathically turning into the companion animal, to discover details about behavior problems, thoughts, and fears. Most pet psychics work with all animals on an intuitive level by tuning into their energy, so that animals do not have to be present for a successful reading.

Pet psychics can help owners and pets better understand and appreciate each other, assess health issues and pinpoint current and future problems, help understand and resolve behavior problems, and clear up any misunderstandings and confusion. Pet psychics typically also can ease the pet's transition into spirit at the end of its life and help the owner handle other end-of-life issues, enhance the performance for working or competition animals, and dis-

cover details of the pet's life before joining a family. Many pet psychics also can help an owner connect with or communicate with pets that have died, and help owners understand what's important in a pet's life.

Typically, the pet owner makes an appointment with the pet psychic for a phone consultation, which usually lasts for about a half hour per pet. The owner has ready

AT A GLANCE

Salary Range

You'll typically set your own rates depending on what the market will bear, but typically the rate may range from $20 to $35 for 15-minute sessions to $75 for an hour's taped session.

Education/Experience

Although no formal education is required to be a pet psychic, there are lots of classes you can take in meditation, relaxation, breathing skills, self-hypnosis, and many other courses in the psychic area.

Personal Attributes

A pet psychic should be empathetic, love animals, have a good sense of intuition and people, and have a deep interest in helping animals and their owners.

Requirements

The ability to intuit or to be sensitive to animals, along with significant psychic ability. Most pet psychics are self-employed, so you'll need good business and marketing skills and good self-management abilities. Most pet psychics are booked weeks in advance, and so must be able to keep accurate records and maintain bookings.

Outlook

There is a tremendous interest in animals in this country and a passion to better understand them, so the outlook for anyone skilled in interpreting pet behavior is expected to remain strong.

a list of questions, along with a description of the pet and the pet's name and age. The pet psychic listens to the problems and then telepathically "connects" with the pet, passing on any helpful information to the pet owner.

Competent professional pet psychics will make sure their clients understand that a reading is never a substitute for qualified veterinary care, and that any animal in need of urgent medical care should always be taken first to a veterinarian. However,

"Mary,"* pet psychic

When they think of a psychic, some people imagine an exotic old woman in a turban with long dangling earrings and a foreign accent, but in Mary's case that couldn't be further from the truth. A corporate secretary by day in a conservative rural Pennsylvania area, Mary couldn't be more down-to-earth. Mary says she uses her natural psychic abilities, compassion, and a down-to-earth communication style to bring pets and their people closer together. Holding down a full-time job, Mary handles her psychic clients after hours and on the weekends. A gifted psychic and medical intuitive, she communicates telepathically in pictures, thoughts, feelings, and words with all species of animals, both living and in spirit.

Typically, clients give her the name, age, and description of their pet over the telephone, and Mary "tunes in" to the animal and reports what the creature is feeling or experiencing. She's particularly gifted at sensing an animal's physical problems, she says.

For example, she's worked with many clients whose cats refused to use the litter box. "Put a litter box in the bedroom," she told one pet owner recently. "She's getting too old to go downstairs to use the box, and she says she'd appreciate one in the bedroom." Sure enough, as soon as the owner placed a litter box in the second floor bedroom where the cat slept, the litter box problem disappeared.

Separation anxiety is another common problem that Mary handles, especially among dogs, who are often tightly bonded to their human family. One client family had boarded their young golden retriever at a highly reputable kennel before going off on a two-week vacation across the country. After one week, the clients called Mary for an emergency reading, because the kennel was reporting that the dog had suddenly fallen into a deep depression and was refusing to get up, much less go outside. After Mary "tuned in" to the dog, she explained to the frantic owners that the dog thought she had been abandoned. Mary sent a soothing telepathic reassurance to the dog that her owners were indeed coming back, and instructed the owners to send loving thoughts to the dog explaining that they would return in five days. "I told them to imagine five sunsets," she explains, because of course, dogs can't tell time. When the clients called the kennel the next day to check on the dog, the kennel owner reported in amazement that the dog experienced a complete turnaround the night before—at exactly the same time that the psychic had sent her message. The dog, the kennel reported, had suddenly jumped up and reverted to normal. The kennel owner was mystified, since the owners chose not to mention the psychic intervention. "They had no idea about any psychic intervention," the owner told Mary, "but our dog showed an incredible improvement within minutes of your sending a message to the dog."

*Not her real name.

pet psychics can work with a vet to relay an animals' feelings and symptoms as the psychic perceives them, but pet psychics do not diagnose, treat, or heal illness or disease in any way (unless they are also licensed veterinarians).

Pitfalls

There are many people who may not be open to the idea of psychic ability, and will react to your career with negativity, ranging from mirth or scorn to downright hostility. In some locales there may be specific laws relating to psychic counseling that must be carefully followed to avoid breaking the law.

Perks

It's possible to make quite a good living doing this work, and if you truly love animals, then helping pet owners better understand their pets—and helping pets better understand the wants and needs of their owners—can be fulfilling. Because many pets are put to sleep each year because of behavioral problems, being able to solve these kinds of problems and repair the human-animal bond can be enormously helpful to both owner and pet.

Get a Jump on the Job

Most pet psychics say they knew from a very early age that they had the ability to connect with animals. Spend time learning how to meditate, to tune in to or connect with animals, and work with all kinds of pets. Read widely in the field and take any related courses that you can find, in meditation, self-hypnosis, or developing psychic ability.

PET PSYCHOLOGIST

OVERVIEW

When Princess Anne's English bull terrier Florence flew into a frenzy and fatally attacked one of the Queen's favorite corgis—along with a maid unfortunate enough to be standing nearby—the terrier was reportedly taken to be examined by a pet psychologist.

The members of the English royal family aren't the only ones who turn to animal behavior consultants when the going gets tough. More and more Americans are also discovering the benefit of understanding a bit more about what's going on in those tiny furry heads. Maybe you've got a cat who suddenly stops using its litter box, or a dog that rips up every tissue in the house as soon as its owner leaves for work. Maybe your ferret looks depressed, your turtle won't come out of its shell, or your bird is pulling out all its feathers. Each of these cases is a behavioral problem that a pet psychologist can help identify and treat.

Pet psychologists (also known as animal behavior counselors) apply their knowledge of animal psychology to diagnose and treat all kinds of behavioral problems in animals, such as aggression, phobias, livestock or car chasing, excessive barking, anxiety, control, and housebreaking issues. Pet psychologists are usually referred by vets to work with owners having problems with domestic pets such as dogs, cats, birds, rabbits, and horses.

Typically, a consultation usually takes between 90 minutes and two hours. At the first visit, which often takes place in the animal's home, the pet psychologist meets with an animal and its owners.

AT A GLANCE

Salary Range

Beginning pet psychologists can expect to earn at least $40,000; an experienced pet psychologist who practices at several clinics or is in private practice might earn more than $60,000 a year.

Education/Experience

Most pet psychologists have advanced degrees, usually in behavior, veterinary medicine, psychology, or a biological science. Many have PhDs and a veterinary degree. Earning such advanced degrees requires a very good undergraduate background, good grades, high motivation, and hard work. Many colleges and universities in North America offer graduate training programs in animal behavior. Experience in working with animals is also helpful.

Personal Attributes

Pet psychologists need to have patience, confidence, empathy, love of animals, and an enjoyment in working with difficult or problem animals, plus the ability to work with humans. They need excellent people skills and good observational skills, as well as assessment and computer skills.

Requirements

You should love animals and be good at science and biology, with good oral and written communication skills. You should be good with people, and be patient and sympathetic. A good head for business and accounts, plus management and business skills, are imperative. Pet psychologists who are self-employed or who run a small business will often need to file "Doing Business As" (DBA) papers and tax forms, and acquire any other permits required under local and/or state ordinances. They may also be required to carry insurance and be bonded.

Outlook

The pet psychology field is small, although the number of pet behavior counselors is growing. A growing interest in animal welfare in the general public may have a positive effect for pet psychologists.

David Spiegel, D.V.M., pet psychologist

What causes a cat to viciously attack your arm? Why would a yellow lab puppy insist on digging up every flower that was just planted? Why does a kitten insist on using the bathtub for a litterbox?

These are all questions that Dr. David Spiegel has encountered in his career as a pet psychologist—a veterinarian whose unique practice is limited exclusively to the prevention and treatment of behavioral problems in animals. Traditionally, most of Dr. Spiegel's patients have been seen privately as house call appointments. Other cases are conducted as phone consultations, and now Dr. Spiegel also sees patients at his office in Swarthmore, Pennsylvania.

"I grew up with a collection of little plastic animals of all kinds," Dr. Spiegel recalls, "My room and bed were adorned with a variety of stuffed animals, and animal pictures were hung and taped upon my walls. As far back as I can remember, I think I always wanted to be a vet."

As an undergraduate, Dr. Spiegel majored in the biological basis of behavior, which included courses from multiple departments, such as psychology, biology, sociology, and anthropology. His favorite classes featured behavioral medicine, the psychology of personal growth, and animal communication. As a senior, he volunteered with Victoria Voith, then-director of the Behavior Clinic at the Veterinary Hospital of the University of Pennsylvania. A vet with a degree in comparative psychology, she was one of the founders of the field of clinical companion animal behavior.

After working with Dr. Voith for a year and a half, "Vickie essentially took me under her wing and became my mentor," Dr. Spiegel recalls. This experience solidified his desire to focus on behavioral therapy after earning his veterinary degree. After graduation from vet school, he hung out his behavioral therapy shingle in 1993, and began writing columns about animal behavior for the *Sunday Delaware News Journal* and the *Philadelphia Inquirer*. Six years later, he moved his practice to Swarthmore, Pennsylvania.

Most of his initial consultations were still scheduled as house calls, since it's best to observe animals in their home environment. "I travel within an hour's radius, which covers Delaware, northeastern Maryland, southern New Jersey, and southeastern Pennsylvania. In certain situations I do travel outside of this area to see cases." It's a large area, and Dr. Spiegel's day often lasts from 9:30 a.m. to 9:30 p.m., Monday through Friday.

"Most of my cases come to me as referrals from more than 50 veterinary hospitals in the region," he says, "in addition to referrals from area shelters, obedience schools, and word of mouth from clients I have served."

What concerns him most is still the safety and happiness of animals, and the best part of his job, he says, is saving animals that might otherwise be destroyed if their behavioral problems had not been resolved. "I have created a highly specialized niche for myself," he says, "along with many others whose lives are devoted to service in this global community."

Taking notes about the specific problem, including relevant medical information, the pet psychologist watches and handles the animal to determine its response to particular situations. Some problems are quite straightforward—(such as a dog terrified of thunderstorms)—and some more complex (such as a cat that won't use its litter box). The psychologist determines what is influencing the animal's behavior, and then develops a treatment plan for the owners to carry out. This may include adjusting the animal's environment to manage difficult behavior. Back at the office, the pet psychologist writes a report outlining the recommended treatment for the owner to follow. Subsequent consultations are important, so that the pet psychologist can assess progress and—when necessary—alter the treatment plan.

In addition, pet psychologists may hold classes for people and their pets, teach at universities, and give speeches or workshops to the general public, media, and schools. Some experts may be involved in court cases or work with animal abuse professionals.

Many pet psychologists specialize in one type of animal and most are self-employed. A few work for animal welfare charities; others work in schools of veterinary medicine, in vet hospitals, or for private consulting firms. Some have a Ph.D. from an animal behavior program, while others have a doctor of veterinary medicine (D.V.M.) degree with additional training in behavior.

In addition to knowledge about animal behavior, pet psychologists should be good at managing a business, since many run an independent practice. Many pet psychologists also offer animal training services.

Pitfalls

Owning your own practice can lead to burnout if you don't have sufficient back-up, and it can be difficult dealing with owners who will not or cannot understand the solution to their pets' problems.

Perks

If you love animals and are fascinated by animal behavior, it can be rewarding to study animal behavior and try to figure out how to solve certain problems. Owning your own business can give you a lot of independence, and the income is usually fairly good.

Get a Jump on the Job

Read as much as you can about animals, learn to understand them, and volunteer in kennels, your vet's office, or your area's humane or animal rescue league even before you graduate. This will give you a good idea about whether you'd like to do this kind of work for a living. Once you're in college, look for internship positions—these are extremely important. Take all the psychology and related courses you can, and talk to other people who work with animals.

PET SITTER

OVERVIEW

Your family has just bought a new puppy, but the kids are in school and Mom and Dad are at work—and no one has time to come home at lunch to tend to the newest family member. Or your family is going away on vacation and you'd really rather avoid the "silent treatment" you always get after you leave your pet in a kennel. For these situations, many American families have found that hiring a pet sitter to take care of their animals in the home is the best answer.

It's no wonder that the pet-sitting service is one of the fastest growing industries in the country today. More than 60 percent of all households in the United States have some kind of pet—an estimated 110 million cats and dogs, not counting all the hamsters, birds, fish, reptiles, rabbits, and other pets. And according to the American Humane Society, these pets are happiest when they're at home, surrounded by familiar sights, sounds, and smells.

In the past, however, most pet owners had few choices when it came to caring for their animals when they were away from home. They could ask friends or neighbors to watch their pets, which might work for a day or two, but is more of an imposition for more than a week. Professional kennels are possible solutions, although not ideal for every pet. Some pets can't be boarded or left with friends and family if they have chronic health conditions requiring special care, and exotic pets may be more difficult to take care of. Likewise, many people prefer to have their dogs, cats, and other pets in the safety and familiar surroundings of home, rather than an unfamiliar boarding

AT A GLANCE

Salary Range

The sky is the limit for pet sitters; salaries may range from $25,000 a year to more than $100,000 a year. Most pet sitters charge by the half-hour visit. On average, a pet sitter will charge about $15 for one 30-minute visit for one pet, with an extra fee for walking a dog. Most pet sitters charge from $1 to $3 for each additional pet per visit. So, a family with one dog and three cats who need visits twice a day would pay a daily rate of $36 to $48, or a weekly rate of $252 to $336. A pet sitter with eight clients in one week may therefore gross between about $1,680 and $2,688.

Education/Experience

Experience in business, as a veterinary technician, or with animal care is helpful, but there are no specific educational requirements.

Personal Attributes

The most important requirement for becoming a pet sitter is a passion for animals—combined with a good sense of organization and discipline to meet your obligations while avoiding mistakes.

Requirements

The government does not regulate pet sitting and no type of license is required to operate a pet sitting business other than the business licenses described below. Although there is no required licensure, the Pet Sitters International and the National Professional Pet Sitters Association offer optional certification courses. Some states, counties, and/or cities require all businesses to purchase a license; others require no licenses at all. Some require licenses for only certain types or sizes of businesses; some cities require home occupation permits or similar special licenses for home-based businesses. Pet sitter business owners must carry liability insurance to cover expenses in the event of an accident and damage to a client's property, or if the sitter does anything that results in harm to the pets. Most pet sitters also pay the estimated $50 to be bonded.

(continues)

environment. When these pet owners want or need to be away from their home, there is only one solution available: hire a pet-sitting service to come to their homes and take care of their beloved pets while they're away. Some breeds of dogs don't take well to kennel life, and most cats—who are highly territorial—find it extremely stressful to be moved temporarily to kennel life.

As a result, many pet owners have discovered that a new alternative presents the best choice of all—hiring a professional pet sitter to come into the home to care for the pet while the owner is away.

As more and more Americans travel for business and pleasure, they are coming to depend on a variety of domestic services. Most pet owners no longer live near their families, and all too many don't even know their neighbors' names, much less feel comfortable asking them to look in on Fido or Spot.

Pets are an important part of many modern families, and finding good reliable care for them can be a problem. According to the experts, pets prefer a familiar environment, a regular diet and exercise routine, and the personal attention provided by a professional pet sitter. This eliminates the trauma of being transported to and from the kennel, and minimizes exposure to illnesses or parasites. Pets stay in their own homes where they are safe and happy.

In addition, pet sitters can provide extra crime-deterring services, such as bringing in the mail and turning on different lights.

Most pet sitters start out on a small scale as an independent service provider. At the first meeting with the pet owner, the pet sitter discusses the service agreement, which gives the pet sitter the authority to be in the pet owner's home. The document should specify the details of what pet services will be performed, any emergency contacts, detailed pet identification, and the pet's unique habits and special needs. Next, the pet sitter discusses the important routines of the pet's day—eating, sleeping, walking, or playing—and learns about all the major and minor health problems a pet may have, along with detailed information on any medication, and the owner's wishes in case of emergency. The sitter learns where favorite toys are kept, and where a pet's favorite hiding places are to make it easier to find the pet at the pet-sitting visit. The pet sitter also needs to hear about a pet's unusual habits, such as fears (loud noises or thunderstorms), sensitive parts of the body, and so on. For example, some cats hate to be picked up; some dogs dislike having their ears touched but love to have a belly rub. The owner provides written verification of up-to-date vaccinations for the pet (such as a rabies tag on a collar).

If the pet owner wants plants to be watered, the sitter must be told where the plants are located and how often and how much water they should get. Other details (such as lights to be turned on in the evening and off in the morning, or curtains to be opened and closed) should be discussed. Pet sitter and owner also should discuss any other necessary details, such as newspapers and mail to be brought in, or trash to be placed at the curb.

Sue Belford, pet sitter

Sue Belford couldn't imagine a better job than one that allows her to be surrounded by furry friends. "Pet sitting is always something I wanted to do," she says. "I do love animals." But while she'd dreamed of pet sitting, she didn't want to give up her comfortable, well-paying full-time job. "I didn't want to quit and dive into pet sitting," Belford says. But then, after the terrorist attack on the World Trade Center, everything changed. "I worked for a textile company that went under after 9-11," she says. "When I was laid off, I thought: 'What better time to do this?' It was the first of the year, I did my research. I had a lot of business experience and I had some experience in pet care." Once she got bonded and insured, she joined Pet Sitters International for extra help with training and all kinds of educational programs, plus a yearly conference.

Today, she is the owner of Happy Paws Pet Sitting, with an office worker and another employee; she's also ready to hire two more sitters to help. Her coverage area includes all of Berks County, Pennsylvania, plus parts of two neighboring counties. Referrals come from her Web site (http://www.happypawspetsittingpa.com), her local vet, and her large boxed Yellow Pages ad.

"I love being my own boss," she says, "and I love all the pets, bonding with them. It's so neat." She's especially attached to her "dailies," the pets who she takes care of five days a week while their owners are at work, giving them an extra walk or a "potty break." "The daily jobs, you get so attached to them," she says. "I love that. Pets to me are very comforting, they relieve a lot of stress."

As much as she loves her job, she cautions that pet sitting isn't really as simple as many people assume. "What I don't like are the 14- and 16-hour days," she says. "That would be the days that are very difficult."

If you dream of being a pet sitter, it's important not just to like animals, but to have experience in taking care of them and also to have a good deal of business experience. "There are a lot of long hours," she says. "If you want to make a living at this, you have to be able to work weekends, nights, and holidays. You might want to start out working for another pet-sitting business to gain experience that way and see if you like it.

"The sky is the limit with what you can earn," she says. "I really feel this field is growing more and more."

Each day when the owner is away, the pet sitter visits the home to feed, care for, and play with the pet (usually twice a day). Pet sitters should be bonded, have commercial liability insurance coverage, and be willing to provide references.

Taking care of pets is only part of the business, however. You'll want to market your pet sitting services through pet-related businesses in your community such as veterinarians, pet supply retailers, dog trainers, and pet grooming services. Remember, many people also hire pet sitters for short periods of time—a weekend away, a night out, a quick lunchtime visit for a new puppy, or time off for family events. Therefore, you may want to develop fee schedules for long- and short-term jobs.

Eventually, if you're really serious about boosting your business, you can plan to expand, hiring extra pet sitters for backup and to enlarge the territory.

Pitfalls

Pet sitting businesses can involve long hours, because pets always have to eat and exercise, whether you feel like it or not. You can expect to be on call 365 days a year, especially during holidays, weekends, and summer months. Some sitters who don't plan well or who don't have backup staff can burn out from the constant responsibility.

Perks

Pet sitting allows people who love animals and who want to run their own business to do so—while earning a very good living and having fun. There's very little up-front money or expensive inventory required to start this business—just gas and a reliable car, a phone line, office supplies such as business cards and flyers, liability insurance, and a business license if your area requires one.

Get a Jump on the Job

Call other pet sitters in the area and see if they would be willing to consult with you and serve as your mentor, perhaps for a small fee. Volunteer at a kennel, animal shelter, or a vet's office to get used to taking care of a variety of pets.

PETTING ZOO OPERATOR

OVERVIEW

For most youngsters who haven't grown up on a farm, a petting zoo provides the perfect opportunity to interact with fluffy sheep, goats, donkeys, chickens, piglets, calves, and llamas—and in many cases, getting right in on the action by climbing right into the pens.

Petting zoos are popping up in some pretty unlikely locations these days. They're showing up at private homes, schools, day care centers, nursing homes, rehabilitation centers, business events, camps, parks, and nature centers—just about anywhere you can imagine. They're popular at block parties, family reunions, festivals, fairs, grand openings, corporate picnics, family-oriented class reunions, and at other occasions.

More and more people are getting interested in petting zoos because it's a harmless entertainment widely recognized as a pleasant, inexpensive, family-friendly activity that can be enjoyed by people of all ages. And because animals are also therapeutic, petting zoos are considered to be ideal for the elderly, people with emotional disorders, or those with physical or mental disabilities.

Yet there's more to owning and running a petting zoo than meets the eye, and it can be more complicated than you might have thought. First, you'll need to figure out where you're going to keep them. Will your zoo be located on your own property, or will you take it on the road? If you have facilities to house them on your property, it will be much more convenient to care for them and less expensive than

AT A GLANCE

Salary Range

Salaries for petting zoo operators vary tremendously, depending on whether the zoo is a full-time or part-time venture, the area in which you operate, the type of clientele you have, and other factors. Someone running a petting zoo as a full-time endeavor who can operate year round can expect to earn between $20,000 and $40,000 a year.

Education/Experience

There are no particular educational requirements to operate a petting zoo. You should, however, have excellent knowledge of the animals you work with, and business expertise, as well. A degree in a subject such as animal husbandry may be useful.

Personal Attributes

You should love animals and enjoy being around them and working with them. You need to be in fairly good physical shape to be able to load and unload animals from trucks and trailers. It helps to be even-natured and patient, because you'll often find yourself working around excited children.

Requirements

Anyone who exhibits certain animals, including goats, sheep, pigs, and rabbits, must be licensed by the United States Department of Agriculture (USDA). You may need other permits, registrations, and licenses as well, but those would vary depending on where you live.

Outlook

The number of jobs in this type of work is expected to increase about as quickly as average through 2012.

renting barn space. If people will come to you, you'll need to make sure you have enough space and the proper facilities. If you decide that you want to run a traveling petting zoo, you'll need to provide

Jon Lawson, petting zoo operator

Jon Lawson's family-run, mobile petting zoo puts him in some pretty interesting situations, including everything from county fairs to corporate America.

Summer and fall are the family's busiest times, when they'll pack up their petting zoo and take off for a five-day stint at a fair or carnival. They spend four days twice a year providing pet zoo services in the grandstand area at NASCAR events, and are popular all year-round at birthday parties and other events. This year, the Lawsons will take their petting zoo to a large corporation's holiday party in a Washington, D.C., hotel, where the animals will get to hang out in the ballroom.

They market their business creatively, encouraging car dealers, shopping center managers, and downtown shop owners to attract customers with a petting zoo. Lawson insists that petting zoos are perfect for street fairs, customer appreciation events, grand openings, family-day events, and picnics.

With a collection of animals including miniature horses, alpacas, baby-doll sheep, Shetland sheep, potbellied pigs, pygmy and Nigerian dwarf goats, giant Flemish rabbits (weighing in at about 22 pounds), chickens, turkeys, ducks, and chicks and ducklings, Lawson's fees vary, depending on the type of event and what equipment is needed. A fair or carnival, for instance, requires that a large tent be set up to protect the animals from the heat and possibility of rain. Prices for birthday parties are less than those for corporate events.

Lawson, who has been in business for six years, says it's very important to find out what sorts of licenses and permits you need, because it varies from location to location. If you're going to exhibit your animals, you'll need to have the USDA exhibition license, in addition to the regular USDA license necessary just to house certain animals.

While he very much enjoys his work, Lawson says that running a petting zoo is physically and mentally demanding.

"There's a lot to deal with," he says. "You're handling animals all the time—loading them and unloading them from trucks and trailers. You're dealing with time constraints, and people, and all kinds of factors. It's not as easy as it looks."

Lawson advises anyone interested in running a petting zoo that it is a labor of love. You can make a living, he says, but chances are you won't get rich.

"You've got to do it because you really enjoy it and want to do it," he says. "That's got to be your primary motivation."

adequate transportation for the animals. You'll also need to investigate the legal aspects of your new business, checking out any zoning regulations for your area.

Once these details have been ironed out, it's time to figure out what animals you'd like to include. Of course, starting a petting zoo is easiest for those who already have access to animals. If you live on a farm or you know someone who raises animals, you'll already be a step ahead of someone who must go out and locate a variety of animals. You may choose to feature a great variety of animals, or may concentrate on just several, but in any case it's a good idea to have a variety of ages. Hardly anyone can resist cuddling a baby chick or a little lamb, particularly if the lamb is being bottle-fed and visitors to the zoo can lend a hand in the feeding.

Some petting zoos also offer pony rides. If you have a pony in your zoo it's a natural combination of services, but you'd need to be sure you had adequate staff to accommodate rides. You don't want to be assisting a child taking a pony ride while leaving six others unattended with Lucy the goat.

Petting zoos have received some bad publicity over the past several years, as they've been linked to illnesses that were thought to have spread from zoo animals to people who had visited the zoos. An *E. coli* outbreak in Florida in March 2005 was linked to cows and calves. As a petting zoo operator, you must be aware of these health issues, and take every precaution to avoid any such problems. An easy way to minimize risk is to provide soap and hot water, and insist that everyone who has contact with the animals wash thoroughly after leaving the pens.

Pitfalls

It can require a significant financial investment if you need to build your zoo and acquire all the animals you need. Because you'll be subject to government regulations, you'll need to find out what the requirements are. In addition, taking care of animals is a 24-hours-a-day, seven-days-a-week job, so you can't think of having a petting zoo as being a part-time job. Even if the petting zoo operates only two days a week, you've got to care for the animals for the other five days as well. If you're counting on a petting zoo for your entire income, you could be in for some lean periods. It's possible to make a living from running a petting zoo, but as a petting zoo owner you're self-employed and responsible for your own medical care and benefits.

Perks

People love petting zoo animals, and generally are happy and excited to be around them, which makes for a pleasant working environment. If you're an animal lover, you'll enjoy spending time with the critters that make up your petting zoo. Generally, you can arrange to have a flexible schedule, or to operate the petting zoo on a part-time basis and pursue other endeavors, as well.

Get a Jump on the Job

Do anything you can to become experienced and comfortable around animals. Volunteer at an animal shelter or hang around other places where you know you'll encounter animals. If there is a petting zoo in your area, ask if you can help during events. Read all you can about animals, and spend as much time around them as you can.

PET WASTE REMOVAL SPECIALIST

OVERVIEW

If you have a pet, you have pet waste to dispose of. While that's not usually a problem for rural folks, pet owners in urban areas and upscale suburbs, parks, and condominiums are another matter entirely. Not only is dog waste messy and stinky, but it also can lead to serious health hazards. Viruses such as the deadly parvo virus, and a whole encyclopedia of worms (round, heart, tape, ring, and whip) all are transmitted through dog feces. For all these reasons, pet waste removal is certainly a job that somebody's got to do—and the owners of a professional pet waste removal service will cart away a family pet's waste weekly, biweekly, or monthly. Believe it or not, you can make a very comfortable living by starting and operating a dog pooper-scooper service in your community. It's fairly easy to begin, requires little investment, no special skills, and minimal equipment to operate. Basically, if you can handle a shovel and a bunch of plastic bags—and you don't mind some off-putting smells in crummy weather—you can run your own pooper-scooper service. (If you'd rather not handle the messy end of the business, you can still get in on this booming business by marketing and managing the service while hiring others to do the dirty work.)

To start, you gather your shovel and bags, make sure you have some reliable transportation, and then spread the word

AT A GLANCE

Salary Range

Earnings vary depending on the size and location of the business, but the average flat monthly fee for one client is between $30 and $60. A pooper-scooper with 100 clients would therefore gross between $36,000 and $72,000 a year.

Education/Experience

No education or experience is required, other than a driver's license.

Personal Attributes

Reliability, honesty, attention to detail, and good business and marketing skills necessary to running a business.

Requirements

Driver's license, reliable transportation, a cell phone, garbage buckets, plastic bags, shovels, gloves, and a good pair of rubber boots. The government does not regulate dog-waste removal, but some states, counties, and/or cities require any individual opening a business to buy a business license; others require no licenses at all. Some locales require licenses for only certain types or sizes of businesses, and some cities require "home occupation permits" or similar special licenses for home-based businesses. Pooper-scooper business owners should carry liability insurance to cover expenses in the event of an accident and damage to a client's property.

Outlook

Because there are more than 63 million pet-owning households in the United States alone, that's a lot of potential poop to scoop. There is enough potential business to support several poop-scooping services in most communities.

about your pooper-scooper service by advertising in local newspapers, pinning fliers to bulletin boards, and advertising through dog-related businesses and clubs in the com-

Jacob D'Aniello, pet waste removal company owner

Jacob D'Aniello was a professional in information technology looking for a career change when he sat down and discussed with his fiancée Susan how to transform their love of animals and the outdoors and their desire for freedom into a new business idea: pet waste removal.

"I always had a paper route," he recalls. "So I tried to think of similar things to do where I could make money." That's when he read about the pet waste removal company. It seemed like a wild idea, but further research revealed dramatic growth in the pet care market. "I had heard of someone doing it in another part of the country," D'Aniello recalls. "I realized no one was doing it in D.C., and it hit me like a ton of bricks." In 2000 he set up an inexpensive Web site and started DoodyCalls with less than $50, in the northern Virginia suburbs. Both D'Aniello and his fiancée kept their full-time jobs so that they could work on their new business at night and on weekends. And then came his big break: "One client purchased a six-month certificate for $500," he says, "and with that money we bought advertising and that jump-started our business."

And so Jacob and Susan jumped into their car with a couple of shovels and some garbage bags and picked up dog waste from homeowner's yards on a twice-weekly, weekly, or biweekly basis. "We had a cardboard box lined with a garbage bag and a trowel," he says.

They promised clients that they would always disinfect tools to eliminate the possibility of spreading diseases, and when the job is finished, they left a bright yellow door hanger so the pet owner knew exactly when the yard was cleaned.

Still, the business didn't take off right away. "When you first start out, your routes aren't dense, so you'll need a car to drive from location to location," D'Aniello says. It's also harder to take vacations as a self-employed scooper. "If you own a business—even if it's only poop—the percentage of people who contract with you are that percentage of the population who do care, which is why they called you. So you can't just go away and come back at your will. It's your source of income."

They slowly began to make a profit. As time went on, they expanded the business to include apartment communities, homeowners associations, and parks, keeping common areas free of pet waste. In addition, they began to sell and maintain "pet waste stations" to provide dog owners with sanitary and convenient places to dispose of pet waste when they walk their dogs.

Demand for DoodyCalls grew steadily, and soon they were hiring employees, buying trucks, and starting to advertise. Business got so good that the two of them were able to quit their jobs to run DoodyCalls full time. "When we started out, I wanted a job where I could work outside," D'Aniello says. "I'd been sitting in a cube for five days a week, and I wanted to breathe some fresh air. I think this is a great job for someone in high school or college to start."

It soon became apparent that DoodyCalls was such a hit that he wouldn't really need to be interviewing for a corporate job again. In 2004, after stories in the *Washington Times* and on MSNBC, their business prospered, and D'Aniello started franchising the business in 2004, and now has franchises in Virginia, Maryland, Boston, and Portland, Oregon. "Selling a franchise isn't like selling a car," D'Aniello says. "When someone buys a franchise, they're obligated to you, and you're obligated to them. It's like a marriage contract for the next 10 years. So you want to be very

munity. Hand out business cards whenever you can; once you get a few clients, word will spread. Each day, you drive around to clients on your list (usually while the owners are away or at work), let yourself into the backyard, and scoop up all the waste you careful who you bring into the system. A good franchise helps to improve the system, because all the franchises affect other franchisees. There are a lot of legal regulations you have to make sure you understand. It's an entirely different beast from running the local company." When investors buy a DoodyCalls franchise, they get a turnkey business, with full-service Internet coverage, e-mail, brochures, collateral pieces, drop-in press releases, manuals about how to run the business, —"everything they need to look like a million bucks from day one," D'Aniello says.

Today D'Aniello handles the franchise side of the business, and his wife handles the administrative side of the scooping business in northern Virginia. Right now DoodyCalls has six employees, five of whom are full time. "We haven't scooped in years," he says, "not because I don't enjoy it. It's just that you're leveraging where you're most valuable."

Of course, there's always the downside to scooping. "Sometimes people haven't cleaned their yards for a very, very long time, and that's not always desirable," he says.

For the right kind of person, a pet waste removal business can be a great occupation. "As a paper boy in Buffalo, New York, I was fairly outdoorsy," he says. "I was used to getting rained on, having cold feet. In this job, you have to be used to bad weather. Just because it's raining and 40 degrees outside— well, you still have to scoop the poop. If you're looking to start this business and weather bothers you, it's not the job for you. You notice the weather a lot more if you have a job that requires you to be out in it."

Other than the rain, snow, and sleet, there is an up side, and D'Aniello has found it. "What I like best is the complete freedom I have now over my schedule," he says. "The first thing is of course freedom, but the second is creativity. I have a lot of creative control, and it's a lot of fun. If I want to work on a press release I can do that. If I want to take a day to learn how to use [a new computer program], or spend a day to go through financial statements, I can. I really enjoy the responsibility and having the opportunity to be creative. In a lot of jobs you're more pigeonholed. Here, I'm in sales, I'm in PR, everything is a lot of fun."

If owning your own pooper-scooper business sounds like fun, D'Aniello advises you to work hard on presenting a professional image. "Everything should look professional or clean, because people are trusting you to come into their yards, to know what days they leave their gate unlocked. A professional image conveys a sense of reliability, so that people believe you'll show up every week.

"People are calling you to perform a service, to try to make their life easier in some way." If they are always calling you to find out if you're coming, or to see if you've been there, you've got a problem." The logistics of coordinating the service exceeds the energy it would take to do the job themselves, he explains. "You need to understand your main job is to make their job easier," he says. "Anything you can do to convince them that you will make their life easier is to your advantage. It's not enough to have a flyer saying you'll pick up their poop."

"For now I'm very happy with DoodyCalls. Susan and I work together, we have wonderful franchises, our local business is growing, and building the franchise system is very challenging," he says. "People don't like picking up dog poop. I don't think they ever will. I've always believed if you can make someone's life just a little bit nicer, there is a service or money that can be made doing it."

can see into the receptacle you've brought, and move on to the next house. Typically, it should take no more than 10 minutes per visit. Most municipalities allow you to dispose of dog manure in their landfills, al-though you'll need to check to make sure.

In 1997 there were probably fewer than 40 dog waste removal services in the entire United States. By early 1999 that number had nearly tripled. Yet still the vast majority of potential markets are not served by any existing pooper-scooper service, and most dog owners are not even aware that services like this exist. Someday it might seem quite normal to have a service that cleans up after your dogs, just as it's not unusual today to use a maid service or a lawn maintenance service.

The oldest dog waste removal service in the United States is Denver's Poop VanScoop; they've been cleaning up after dogs since the late 1970s.

People hire such a service for a number of reasons. First, they don't have time. Two-income families, single-parent households, executives, and professionals work long hours, and when they finally take some time off, the last thing they want to do is to dispose of dog poop. Some people need the service because they have physical limitations. Blind people with guide dogs, handicapped individuals with assistance dogs, sick people, the elderly, and people with disabilities all need help cleaning up after their animals. For some, the availability of a dog waste removal service makes the difference in being able to keep a favorite pet or having to get rid of it.

Then, there's a third reason why people hire waste removal services: the Ick Factor. Many dog owners have all the free time in the world and they're perfectly healthy—but they just don't like to have to deal with dog manure. As one customer told a dog waste removal specialist: "Some things you do for yourself, and some things you pay to have done."

Pitfalls

This can be a smelly, dirty job, especially in the summer. You're also out in all kinds of weather, a lot of it very bad, but the dog waste removal expert must make his or her appointed rounds.

Perks

This is an easy business to start; it requires little investment, no special skills, and minimal equipment to operate. If you work hard, you can be earning good money in no time.

Get a Jump on the Job

It doesn't take a lot of experience to pick up dog doo-doo, but it does take some talent and skill to run your own business. Take as many business-related courses in school as you can, and read widely about how to run your own business. Jobs such as paper routes, lawn-mowing services, and pet-sitting services all can provide great experience in learning how to work with clients and be responsible and professional.

SHEEP SHEARER

OVERVIEW

They're fluffy, they're woolly, they're oh-so-cute—so what's not to like about spending every day with sheep, earning a living by shearing their fleece? An experienced shearer can shear up to 300 sheep a day, and zip through even more lambs. Sheep are found in every state, although they tend to be more highly concentrated in Western states. Texas has more sheep than any other state.

Normally, a shearer will contract with a sheep farmer to shear the entire herd at one go. The sheep are rounded up into a catching pen, and then pulled out one by one to be shorn. Sheep shearers, using handheld, electric shearing machines to which different combs and cutters can be attached, aim to remove the wool in one piece with a set pattern of shearing strokes. Sound easy? It's not. And it's even more difficult if the sheep is frightened or upset and harder to hold. That's why patience and a love of animals is important; sheep shearers who can handle the animals with confidence and reassurance will have an easier job of it in the end.

Unavoidably, sometimes a sheep will be cut during shearing. When that happens, the shearer needs to know how to treat the cut to avoid infection. Also, shearers must be very careful about keeping their cutting instruments clean so that diseases aren't spread among a flock or from farm to farm. Some breeders have invested $1,000 or more in each sheep, and would suffer tremendous financial loss if disease occurred in their flock.

Once the sheep are shorn, they're returned to an area called the letting-out pen, where they can be counted and examined.

AT A GLANCE

Salary Range

The earnings of sheep shearers vary tremendously, depending on the amount of shearing they do and the locations in which they work. Shearers usually are paid for each sheep they shear, which normally ranges between $1.50 and $3 per head. Therefore, salaries can range from a few hundred dollars a week to thousands of dollars, depending on the amount of work available and how much the shearer is willing to do.

Education/Experience

There are no set educational requirements for sheep shearers. There are sheep shearing schools in the United States and other countries, mostly offered through state universities or county extension offices. Sheep shearing courses, which generally last two to three days, are useful in teaching the basics of the job, but most of the training comes on the job.

Personal Attributes

You should have good hand-eye coordination and good concentration skills. Shearing sheep is demanding physical work, so it will help if you're in good shape. You need to be motivated to work, and able to follow instructions and deal with people.

Requirements

Unless you live in an area where there are enough sheep to support your business, you'll need to be willing to travel. In addition to shearing skills, sheep shearers need to have some business skills in order to keep track of billing, paying taxes, and other tasks associated with running a business.

Outlook

Good. The average age of a sheep shearer in the United States is above 50, and many are expected to begin retiring in the next decade. Shearers will be needed to take their place.

Some sheep shearers tend to be nomadic, following the shearing season around the world to find work. Others stay at home

Aaron and Michelle Kaufman, sheep shearers

Michelle Kaufman comes from a sheep shearing family, but her husband Aaron, who grew up in Orange County, California, had never even seen a live sheep before the two met in college. He got hooked on shearing while visiting Michelle's family, and the couple decided to start their own shearing business. "We decided that we wanted to work for ourselves," Michelle says, "and we both enjoy working with animals, so it seemed like a natural move."

The couple moved from California to Ohio, founded Sheep Shearers, Inc., and have been happily shearing sheep ever since. "Shearing is our full-time career," Michelle explains. "It is a seasonal occupation that varies according to the area where you live. In most areas, there is at least some shearing done all year round. It is not, however, always busy enough to earn a living."

When that's the case, Michelle and Aaron take off for other parts of the world, which is typical for professional shearers. This year, they'll spend three months in northern New Zealand, working six days a week shearing sheep with a shearing crew. "Sheep outnumber people there ten to one, so there's lots of work for shearers," Michelle says.

The American West, Australia, Ireland, England, and South Africa also are popular working holiday destinations for sheep shearers.

While sheep shearing classes are useful, Michelle says the real training takes place on the job. "It takes a lot of repetition to get comfortable and reach a professional skill level," she explains.

The largest flock the couple ever was hired to shear included 500 head of lambs, but the average size flock they shear in Ohio is about 30 head. It takes them about four minutes to shear each sheep, but Michelle says that some shearers work much quicker. Shearing tends to be a competitive task, she says, and shearers regularly have contests to determine who is fastest.

If you're interested in sheep and shearing as a career, Michelle suggests that you get some training, and then start out slowly and really learn the trade. "You've got to realize that this job is very physically demanding, and you'll have to start out slow until you build up your stamina," she says.

Once you establish a clientele, she says, you should treat your customers fairly, and do a quality job. "If you stick to it, and you do good work, people are going to ask you to come back," Michelle says. "Sheep farmers are very loyal, and sometimes they will pay a little bit extra just to keep a quality shearer. There is money to be made if you stick to it, and always opportunities for travel all over the world."

and find other work during the off-season. However you choose to work, sheep farmers are happy to find good shearers, so if you work hard and treat the sheep and farmers well, chances are you'll be hired the next time shearing is necessary.

Pitfalls

Because shearing is seasonal work, it can be difficult to find enough work to earn a full-time living. Shearers are responsible for providing their own equipment, which requires a financial investment to start out.

Perks

Sheep shearers are able to work independently, which is appealing to many people, and it's a lucrative business, so if you're willing to work long days and travel for work during the off-season, you can make a comfortable living. If you like travel, you'll love this job; most sheep shearers travel fairly extensively, some leaving home for months at a time to find work in other regions, other countries, or even a different continent. You're your own boss and can make your own hours.

Get a Jump on the Job

Get used to being around sheep and learn how to handle them. If you live near a sheep farm, ask if you can watch as the animals are being shorn. Read all you can about sheep shearing and talk to a shearer, if possible.

WILDLIFE REHABILITATOR

OVERVIEW

If you've ever found a fledgling bird who fell out of its nest, an injured deer, or a disturbed nest of baby rabbits, you may well have wondered to whom you could turn to help take care of the animals. Most vets won't care for wildlife—and that's where the wildlife rehabilitator comes in.

Wildlife rehabilitators treat and care for animals that have been injured, are sick, or have been displaced or orphaned. They also may rescue and rehabilitate animals that have been illegally sold or trafficked. They undertake a wide variety of tasks, and job descriptions vary depending on the type of facility in which you'd work, and whether or not there are other rehabilitators to help.

Wildlife rehabilitators typically spend their time capturing and transporting injured animals, feeding baby birds and animals, and making sure that baby and wounded animals get enough to eat and drink. They also tend to wounds and injuries, clean cages, and log information about the care of the animals. Then there's time spent ordering supplies, giving educational talks about wild animals, fund-raising, promoting rehabilitation shelters, locating and applying for grant money, and trying to raise private funds to support the work. While animals typically are tended to in a wildlife rehabilitation center, rehabilitators often take animals home to provide round-the-clock care.

Educating the public about wildlife is a very important part of a wildlife rehabilitator's job. You're likely to find yourself answering a lot of questions from people who find injured wildlife—especially: "Can I keep it?" (The answer to that question should always be no.)

AT A GLANCE

Salary Range

Many rehabilitators are unpaid volunteers, while others work in internships that offer a stipend. An experienced rehabilitator with a college degree can expect to earn up to $30,000 a year.

Education/Experience

Although there are no specific educational requirements for this job, a college degree in biology or ecology, with emphasis on ornithology, ecology, or animal behavior, is recommended.

Personal Attributes

In addition to having a genuine love and concern for wildlife, you should be flexible, able to make sound decisions quickly, and able to work as a team player. You should have good listening and speaking skills and be able to deal with many types of people. Also, animal rehabilitation is not a nine-to-five job, so you should be willing to work long and sometimes erratic hours.

Requirements

Wildlife rehabilitators in the United States are required to have state and federal permits. You may need additional permits from local agencies, as well. However, if you work with a licensed rehabilitator or in a licensed facility, you may be covered by that license and not need one of your own. Specific permits, such as a wildlife transport permit, also may be necessary. Professional wildlife rehabilitators are expected to meet the minimum standards for wildlife rehabilitation, as approved by the National Wildlife Rehabilitators Association and the International Wildlife Rehabilitation Council.

Outlook

Animal rehabilitator jobs are expected to grow about as fast as average through 2012. Demand for these jobs is expected to remain steady as communities are increasingly recognizing the value of wild animals and the problem of animal abuse.

Suki Kermes, wildlife rehabilitator

For Suki Kermes, taking care of wild animals is a dream come true. Kermes is the clinical supervisor at Wildlife Rescue and Rehabilitation, located in the Texas hill country west of Austin and San Antonio. "I could not ask for a job that I'm more suited for, mentally, philosophically, and physically," Kermes says. "This job is more my life's work than just a so-called job."

Like most wildlife rehabilitators, Kermes grew up around animals. "I have always loved animals and known that I wanted to fill my life with their presence," she says. "I always had dogs and cats while I was growing up, and I loved being outside and exploring. I grew up riding and working with horses, and that really built the foundation for my drive to work with animals. I could not imagine my life not being surrounded by animals."

She enjoys every day at the wildlife rehabilitation center, even though no two days are alike. "You never know what to expect out of each day, except that you'll be amazed by these wondrous animals on a daily basis," Kermes says. Her job includes many aspects of animal care, including preparing specially formulated diets for each animal, and cleaning the animals and their surroundings. She administers medicines and helps with medical treatment and surgeries, answers the center's 24-hour hotline, spends hours observing injured animals and preparing them for release, and rescues wounded animals.

Although every animal must be treated differently, the philosophy of care is the same. "The absolutes we have established for the animals are to do what is most ethical and best for each one, ensure their safety and overall well-being, and to view the living conditions from the animal's perspective," she says. "We provide clean bedding, water, and housing at all times, and strive to be compassionate and to provide respect and dignity for all animals."

One of Kermes' most rewarding experiences at the rehabilitation center was her work with a young gray fox that had been attacked and injured by a large dog. The fox was young, just weaned, and when he arrived at Wildlife Rescue and Rehabilitation, he was covered with puncture wounds all over his head and face. "Most places would have taken one look at him and labeled him a goner, but our vet tech and I knew otherwise," Kermes says. "This little fox was such a fighter, you could just tell that he wanted to live. So, we took him home the first few nights and provided intensive supportive therapy, tube-fed him, and built up his strength." Then the fox was sent to a vet specialist in San Antonio who agreed that it was worthwhile to give it a shot and perform reconstructive surgery on his face. "Long story short, he was released four months later to a protected area," Kermes says.

One of the most important aspects of rehabilitating wildlife is to be able to separate yourself from the animal, Kermes says, and to make your decisions based on what's best for the animal, not yourself. Kermes, who has a degree in environmental studies and anthropology with a minor in biology, got an internship during college with the Audubon Zoo in New Orleans. She then worked at a small zoo near Philadelphia, but knew that wildlife rehabilitation was her real passion.

Anyone interested in becoming a wildlife rehabilitator should get some experience by volunteering or working as an intern at a facility that treats or shelters animals, she recommends. "Get your foot in the door early," Kermes says. "Only experience working with animals is really going to get you anywhere. Volunteer at your local Humane Society, and look into internships or volunteer programs with wildlife. Read as much as you can about animals. All of this will help you have an understanding of what animals need, who they are, and why they act the way they do."

While you might think that jobs involving the care of wildlife would be found in remote, rural areas, most wildlife rehabilitation centers are located in heavily populated areas. That's because the more interaction between humans and wildlife, the more likely the resulting problems.

Wildlife rehabilitators work for both government agencies and private organizations. Privately run rehabilitation centers almost always operate as nonprofit facilities. In fact, wildlife rehabilitation is by law a nonprofit endeavor, because wildlife rehabilitators in the United States are not permitted to charge for treating wild animals. Environmental educational facilities run by cities, counties, or states are publicly funded.

While it's important for a wildlife rehabilitator to care about the animals he or she treats, it's also imperative that the rehabilitator always remember that the animal is wild, and should remain so. Rehabilitators care for their animals, but in no way should try to train them or make pets out of them. Rehabilitators also must be knowledgeable about the species they treat, understanding their history, habits, and the dangers the animals might present.

Pitfalls

Wildlife rehabilitation can be demanding and frustrating work. People who get into this field typically are true animal lovers, and it can be upsetting to deal with animals that have been hurt—sometimes intentionally. In addition, because most privately funded animal rehabilitation facilities are nonprofit organizations, jobs may be limited due to minimal funds available.

Perks

Rehabilitating wildlife is enormously rewarding. Many people, in fact, rehabilitate animals without being paid, just because they enjoy the work and find it to be very satisfying. Caring for injured or displaced wild animals is truly a labor of love, and no two days will be the same.

Get a Jump on the Job

The best way to get some experience in this field is to volunteer at a facility such as a wildlife refuge or rehabilitation center. If there's no such facility in your area, start by volunteering at your local pet shelter or zoo. Watch nature films and documentaries to learn about the habits and habitats of wild animals, and read all you can about wildlife and wildlife rehabilitation.

ZOOKEEPER

OVERVIEW

Most of us have spent pleasant summer afternoons at a zoo, mimicking monkeys, staring at giraffes, and laughing at the antics of the giant pandas, but we don't usually think about the one person whose awesome job it is to be responsible for all these creatures—the zookeeper.

Today's zoos are really dedicated to acting as conservation and educational centers, serving the needs of both animals and humans. Working closely together, zoos around the world operate captive breeding programs for animals considered to be in danger of extinction, and help to maintain healthy populations. Good zoos now offer a comprehensive range of educational facilities so that they can play a vital role in teaching the public about the threat facing the world's wildlife. Therefore, the work of today's zoos—and the keepers employed there—is extremely important.

Zookeepers are responsible for overseeing the daily care of animals in zoos, including tasks such as preparing food and feeding, cleaning up after, bathing, and grooming animals. They work with animal nutritionists, environmentalists, curators, and zoo animal caretakers to make sure the animals receive the proper care and are in comfortable and advantageous environments. They also administer medications, attend to animal births, play with animals, and perform other tasks. Zookeepers try to get to know the animals they're responsible for, since knowing the habits and personalities of the animals make it easier to notice problems and potential problems such as an illness or injury.

AT A GLANCE

Salary Range

Zookeepers' salaries range from about $28,000 to start to about $50,000. Salaries are based on the experience and education of the zookeeper, and vary depending on the location of the zoo, how the zoo is funded, and other factors.

Education/Experience

You'll need at least an associate or bachelor's degree in an area such as biology, zoology, or animal science. Many zoos look for zookeepers with master's or doctorate degrees.

Personal Attributes

You'll need to enjoy working around animals and have a respect for them and their environments. You need to be responsible and dedicated to the job, because the animals depend on you for their well-being. You should be organized, have a neat appearance, be able to accept suggestions, and have the ability to work with others. You also should have good communication skills, as zoo guests will ask you about the animals and their habits.

Requirements

Requirements will vary, depending on the employer. Some zoos require criminal background checks, drug testing, or other screenings. Continuing education probably will be required.

Outlook

While jobs for the overall category of animal care and service workers is expected to increase at a rate that is faster than average, jobs for zookeepers are relatively few and far between, and will continue to be very competitive.

In some larger zoos, a keeper will care for just one type of animal, such as large cats, primates, or pachyderms. Small zoos usually require zookeepers to care for many types of animals. Some zookeepers, especially those who specialize in working with

Catherine Vitale, zookeeper

Catherine Vitale knew from the time she was a little girl that someday she'd have a job working with animals. When she was five years old, she and her father were visiting a zoo when a sheep from one of the exhibits ran into her and knocked her down. She picked herself up, undaunted, and decided that her career would definitely involve caring for animals. "Ever since that day, I knew I would work with animals in some way."

Vitale kept her dream of caring for animals alive through a series of internships and research projects. During her sophomore year of high school, she was selected as a teen intern at the Bronx Zoo in New York. During the internship period, she participated in educational classes and learned to care for the animals in the children's zoo and the camel barn.

In the summers before her junior and senior years of college, she served as an intern at the Queens Zoo, where she assisted the zookeepers with their various duties. She also participated in field research during her college career at the University of Rhode Island, helping to immobilize white-tailed deer so that they could be fitted with radio collars that would record their home ranges.

Vitale graduated from college with a bachelor's of science degree in wildlife biology and management. The degree, coupled with her past experiences, contributed to her success in landing a full-time job as a zookeeper in the mammal department of the Bronx Zoo, where she has worked for more than four years.

Her job entails a series of tasks, including feeding, cleaning up after, training, and generally caring for a variety of animals, including elephants and tigers. On a typical day, she begins by checking all the animals in her care to make sure they've fared well during the night.

"I look to see if they went to the bathroom overnight, ate all of their food, and I check to make sure they look healthy," she says.

It's also her job to clean the animals' exhibit areas and let the animals out into the exhibits so the public can see them. While the animals are in the exhibit areas, Vitale cleans their night holding areas, and then spends the rest of the day providing information to zoo visitors and preparing food that meets the particular dietary needs of each animal.

She also trains the animals to perform basic behaviors, such as lying down, approaching the zookeepers, and opening their mouths. These behaviors make it easier for zookeepers and veterinarians to care for the animals.

Once the zoo closes, Vitale moves the animals back to their night holding areas and prepares their dinners. While the work may sound routine, Vitale says that every day brings new opportunities and challenges.

Vitale thoroughly enjoys her work, relishing the opportunity to spend time around a variety of mammals. "The best part of the job is the animals," she says. "I get to work with exotic animals that I may never get to see in the wild."

Vitale advises anyone interested in becoming a zookeeper to get all the experience you can working with animals in any capacity, such as volunteering at an animal shelter, a zoo, or with a veterinarian, or working on a farm. "Zookeeping can be a lot like farm work," she says, "so experience on a farm also is great.

"One of the great things about being a zookeeper is that no day is ever typical," she says. "There's always something new to learn."

just one type of animal, also may be involved in research on that type of animal.

Zookeepers are friends to the animals they care for, and need to be able to establish a trusting relationship in order to work with them effectively. Zookeepers and animals spend a lot of time together, and get to know one another very well.

Don't think, however, that the work of a zookeeper is restricted to cleaning and feeding the animals. There's lots of paperwork: Zookeepers must keep daily records of feeding, illness, births, behavior changes, and so forth. They also may need to be available to lead educational programs, and visit schools, do public speaking, and even come up with behavior modification strategies. Other job functions include exhibit maintenance, construction, and heavy equipment operating.

Pitfalls

Zookeeping is a tough field to break into, because there are a relatively few number of jobs available. Zoos typically receive 200 to 300 applications for each zookeeper position posted. You may need to work as an assistant until a zookeeper's job becomes available, and be willing to relocate in order to get a position. Because competition for zookeeper positions is keen, the pay is lower than for some comparable jobs. Another potential downside to being a zookeeper is that, just like people, animals sometimes get sick or injured, and

sometimes die. That can be very difficult for zookeepers, who tend to get quite attached to the animals they care for. In addition, the paperwork and administrative tasks that are part of the job can be frustrating for some zookeepers, who would prefer to spend all their time caring for and working with the animals.

Perks

A zoo environment can be lots of fun, and most zookeepers find their work very rewarding. Being a zookeeper provides a wonderful opportunity to gain intimate knowledge of the animals and their behavior. You'll learn how they react to different situations and experiences. Most zookeepers also find it particularly rewarding to assist with births.

Get a Jump on the Job

Try to get some hands-on experience working with animals. You could volunteer at a zoo, wildlife rehabilitation center, or an animal shelter. A few zoos offer part-time and seasonal employment; some also offer internships. Any experience working with animals will help you when applying for a position. Visit a zoo near you and see if you can talk to a zookeeper; they often are available to answer questions and provide information. Learn all you can about animals by reading and watching television shows and documentaries about animals.

APPENDIX A. ASSOCIATIONS, ORGANIZATIONS, AND WEB SITES

ANIMAL BEHAVIORIST

Animal Behavior Society
Indiana University
2611 East 10th Street, #170
Bloomington, IN 47408-2603
(812) 856-5541
aboffice@indiana.edu
http://www.animalbehavior.org

Founded in 1964, the Animal Behavior Society (ABS) has a mission to encourage and promote the study of animal behavior. The nonprofit organization is open to anyone interested in animal behavior. Members receive a monthly scholarly journal, a quarterly newsletter, membership lists, educational opportunities, and can attend annual and regional meetings. The ABS certifies animal behaviorists and provides (for a fee) career counseling for people who are studying, or are interested in studying, to be an animal behaviorist.

International Association of Animal Behavior Consultants
505 Timber Lane
Jefferson Hills, PA 15025
jlrhoover@comcast.net
http://www.iaabc.org

ANIMAL FORENSIC SPECIALIST

American Academy of Forensic Sciences
PO Box 669
Colorado Springs, CO 80901
(719) 636-1100
reception@aafs.org
http://www.aafs.org

The American Academy of Forensic Sciences (AAFS) was founded more than 50 years ago to represent forensic specialists in all areas. The organization has more than 5,600 members. Its Web site offers advice on forensic careers and education matters. It also contains a "young forensic scientists" forum and an online version of the AAFS newsletter.

U.S. Fish and Wildlife Service National Fish and Wildlife Forensics Laboratory
1490 East Main Street
Ashland, OR 97520
(514) 482-4989
ken_goddard@fws.gov
http://www.lab.fws.gov/index.html

The U.S. Fish and Wildlife Service's National Fish and Wildlife Forensics Laboratory was established in 1989. Its primary missions are to match pieces, parts, or products of an animal with its species or subspecies; to determine the causes of deaths of animals; and to help wildlife officers find out whether a crime involving an animal has been committed. It also works to identify and compare physical evidence as to how it relates to crime scenes. The laboratory makes some projects available to senior high students on a limited basis. You can find out about these projects by contacting Edgard O. Espinoza, the deputy laboratory director, at ed_espinoza@fws.gov.

ANIMAL SHELTER DIRECTOR

American Humane Association
63 Inverness Drive East
Englewood, CO 80112

(303) 792-9900
http://www.americanhumane.org/site/
PageServer

The American Humane Association tries to prevent cruelty, abuse, neglect, and exploitation of children and animals and to assure that their interests and well-being are fully, effectively, and humanely guaranteed. American Humane envisions a nation where no child or animal will ever be a victim of willful abuse or neglect. As a recognized leader in professional education, training and advocacy, research and evaluation, American Humane joins with other individuals and organizations to make this vision a reality.

Humane Society of the United States
2100 L Street, NW
Washington, DC 20037-1598
http://www.hsus.org

National Animal Control Association
PO Box 480851
Kansas City, MO 64148-0851
http://www.nacanet.org

The National Animal Control Association (NACA) was formed in 1978 for the express purpose of assisting its members to perform their duties in a professional manner. Only carefully selected and properly trained animal control personnel can correct community problems resulting from irresponsible animal ownership. NACA's purpose is to preserve the human-animal bond by insisting on responsible animal ownership. The NACA offers training conferences, a bimonthly magazine, a training academy, and publishes a training guide for animal control personnel.

ANIMAL WRANGLER

International Alliance of Theatrical Stage Employees, Moving Picture Technicians, Artists and Allied Crafts (IATSE)

1430 Broadway, 20th Floor
New York, NY 10018
(212) 730-1770
http://www.iatse-intl.org

With a membership of more than 105,000 members, the IATSE is the largest labor union in the entertainment and related industries, and was formed more than a century ago; animal wranglers who work for the entertainment industry can belong to this organization. IATSE was originally chartered by the American Federation of Labor as the National Alliance of Theatrical Stage Employees in 1893; its name has evolved over the course of 110 years of geographic and craft expansion as well as technological advancement. The current title was adopted in 1995.

International Association of Avian Trainers and Educators
350 St. Andrews Fairway
Memphis, TN 38111
(901) 685-9122
http://www.iaate.org

The International Association of Avian Trainers and Educators (IAATE) was founded to foster communication, professionalism, and cooperation among those individuals working with birds who train, display, research, husband, conserve, and educate. Trainers and other personnel involved in the husbandry and research of birds must have a clear understanding of their individual roles as well as the interplay between themselves, the animals in their care, the communities in which they live and work, and the public which they serve and to which they are ultimately responsible. IAATE will provide opportunities through which bird trainers can exchange and disseminate current knowledge, research and other information among themselves in professional and social settings. In addition, IAATE seeks to maintain a positive public image by preparing its members to act as ambassadors for the avian community.

AQUARIST

American Zoo and Aquarium Association
8403 Colesville Road, Suite 710
Silver Spring, MD 20910
(301) 562-0777
http://www.aza.org

The American Zoo and Aquarium Association (AZA) is a nonprofit organization dedicated to the advancement of zoos and aquarium facilities. It works in the areas of conservation, science, education, and recreation. Founded in 1924, the AZA is managed by a board of directors and has more than 5,500 members. It is the largest zoo and aquarium organization in the world.

The Oceanography Society
PO Box 1931
Rockville, MD 20849
(301) 251- 7708
info@tos.org
http://www.tos.org

The Oceanography Society was founded in 1988 for the purpose of spreading knowledge about oceanography and its applications. The nonprofit organization publishes a magazine covering all aspects of oceanography, provides educational opportunities for members, holds meetings at which members can share research and knowledge, and awards members for outstanding work in the field.

The Wildlife Conservation Society
2300 Southern Boulevard
Bronx, NY 10460
(718) 220-5100
membership@wcs.org
http://www.wcs.org

Headquartered in the world-famous Bronx Zoo, the Wildlife Conservation Society (WCS) works to save wildlife and wild land through education and conservation. It also manages the largest system of urban wildlife parks in the world. In addition to the Bronx Zoo, it manages the New York Aquarium, and the Central Park, Queens and Prospect Park zoos. The WCS Web site contains information about the zoos and aquarium. There are membership, volunteer, and donation opportunities for individuals and corporations.

ASSISTANCE DOG TRAINER

Assistance Dogs International
http://www.adionline.org/default.html

Assistance Dogs International, Inc. is a coalition of nonprofit organizations that train and place assistance dogs. The purpose of ADI is to improve the areas of training, placement, and utilization of assistance dogs as well as staff and volunteer education. Members of ADI meet each year to share ideas, attend seminars, and discuss such things as educating the public about assistance dogs, legal rights, standards and guidelines for training dogs, and improving the utilization and bonding of each team. ADI also publishes a newsletter for members and subscribers.

Assistance Dogs of America
Education and Training Facility
8806 State Route 64
Swanton, Ohio 43558
(419) 285-3622
info@adai.org
http://adai.org

Assistance Dogs of America, Inc. (ADAI) locates, trains, and places special, highly skilled service and therapy dogs with disabled adults and children, helping clients become more independent and providing them with a renewed sense of freedom. For more than 20 years ADAI has been helping the physically challenged, placing more than 150 assistance dogs with clients.

Canine Companions for Independence
PO Box 446
2965 Dutton Avenue
Santa Rosa, CA 95402-0446
(707) 577-1700
info@caninecompanions.org
http://www.cci.org

Canine Companions for Independence (CCI) trains assistance dogs and pairs them with people who have physical and emotional disabilities. Founded in 1975, CCI has placed nearly 2,500 dog-owner teams throughout the country. The nonprofit organization serves the entire country through five regions, and has seven locations. It operates solely on donations, and there is practically no cost to the person who gets the dog. CCI-trained dogs assist people who are deaf or hearing impaired, physically handicapped, and those with emotional problems. The agency welcomes volunteers and is always looking for people to help raise puppies.

Dogs for The Deaf
10175 Wheeler Road
Central Point, OR 97502
(541) 826-9220
http://www.dogsforthedeaf.org

Dogs for the Deaf (DFD) is a nonprofit organization founded in 1977 and dedicated to rescuing and professionally training dogs to assist people and enhance their lives. Hearing dogs are chosen from adoption shelters, where they might otherwise be euthanized. All hearing dogs are trained, placed, and followed for free.

Guiding Eyes for the Blind
611 Granite Springs Road
Yorktown Heights, NY 10598
(914) 245-4024
info@guidingeyes.org
http://www.guidingeyes.org

Guiding Eyes for the Blind has graduated more than 6,000 guide dog teams since it was founded in 1954. The nonprofit organization is funded entirely by donations. It does not receive any government funding. The school, which has paired guide dogs with people from all over the world, is recognized as one of the world's top guide dog schools. There is no cost involved for the person receiving a dog. The organization has many opportunities for volunteer work, and its Web site provides information for someone who wishes to become a guide dog trainer.

Guide Dogs for the Blind: Puppy Raising
(800) 295-4050
http://www.guidedogs.com/puppy.html

National Service Dogs
PO Box 28009 Preston Postal Outlet
Cambridge, ON N3H 5N4
Canada
(519) 662-4223
info@nsd.on.ca
http://www.nsd.on.ca/about.htm

National Service Dogs is a nonprofit Canadian charity specializing in breeding, training, and placing Labrador and golden retrievers with children who have autism. It is the first and only service dog program focused on children with autism in Canada.

DOG DAY CARE OWNER

The American Boarding Kennels Association
1702 East Pikes Peak Avenue
Colorado Springs, CO 80909
(877) 570-7788
http://www.abka.com/abka/

The nonprofit trade association for more than 3,000 pet care service businesses in the United States and around the world. In addition to pet boarding and dog day care, ABKA members offer a variety of services for pets including grooming, training, pet transportation, shipping, pet supplies, food sales, and so on. ABKA offers information, publications, advertising opportunities, education, facility accreditation, meetings, and business networking opportunities

International Association of Canine Professionals
PO Box 560156
Montverde, FL 34756-0156
(407) 469-2008
iac@mindspring.com
http://www.dogpro.org

The International Association of Canine Professionals (IACP) provides resources for people in all aspects of canine care. It promotes professionalism in all areas of canine care, and communication between members. Regional networking opportunities are offered, as well as educational opportunities for members.

DOG GROOMER

GroomTeam USA
http://www.groomteamusa.com

GroomTeam USA is a nonprofit organization that encourages professional pet stylists to make the most of their grooming education and skills, and offers them the chance to represent the United States at World Team Competitions. Team selection is based on points accumulated at various GroomTeam sanctioned contests held throughout the country over a two-year period. GroomTeam sends the top point earners as a team to compete abroad in the Olympics of Pet Styling.

International Association of Canine Professionals
PO Box 560156
Montverde, FL 34756-0156
(407) 469-2008
iac@mindspring.com
http://www.dogpro.org

The International Association of Canine Professionals (IACP) provides resources for people in all aspects of canine care, including dog groomers. It promotes professionalism in all areas of canine care, and communication between members. Regional networking opportunities are offered, as well as educational opportunities for members.

International Society of Canine Cosmetologists (ISCC)
18710 Kelly Boulevard
Dallas, TX 75287
(972) 414-9715

Established in 1990, ISCC is concerned with the continuing education and advancement of professional pet stylists. Dedicated to providing essential communication, networking, continuing education, and certification services, ISCC provides a balanced and varied program of activities at the local, regional, and national level, and covers the latest trends, innovations, and issues facing the industry.

National Dog Groomers Association of America
PO Box 101
Clark, PA 16113

(724) 962-2711
ndga@nationaldoggroomers.com
http://www.nationaldoggroomers.com

The National Dog Groomers Association of America (NDGAA) is a professional membership organization for people in the profession. It promotes the exchange of professional information among its members, and provides educational workshops and seminars. It also sponsors grooming competitions and offers a professional liability program.

DOG HANDLER

Owner Handlers Association
PO Box 353
Nazareth, PA 18064-0353
http://www.canineworld.com/oha

An organization founded to encourage and promote the sport of owner handling and training of purebred dogs, to encourage and promote sportsmanship among purebred dog fanciers, and to provide information about purebred dogs. The Owner Handler Association of America, Inc. includes members from all 50 states, Canada, and Puerto Rico.

Professional Handlers Association
17017 Norbrook Drive
Olney, MD 20832
(301) 924-0089
webmaster@phadoghandlers.com
http://www.phadoghandlers.com

PHA is a trade organization dedicated to representing the interests of professional dog handlers, and furthering the sport of showing dogs throughout the United States. The PHA seeks to promote a beneficial working relationship among members, clients, other handler organizations, and the American Kennel Club.

DOG SHOW JUDGE

International All Breed Canine Association
PMB 234
4742 Liberty Road South
Salem, OR 97302
(503) 316-9860
http://www.iabca.com/index.htm

The International All Breed Canine Association of America (IABCA) began in the late 1990s with the intent of making an International "UCI" Championship Title available to the American public while not exposing the dogs to the danger and inconvenience of international travel. To accomplish this, an association was formed with an international association of dog clubs headquartered in Germany. There are many countries throughout Europe, North America, and the Far East represented in the association. Through this international organization, international titles are awarded to dogs who meet the requirements.

International Association of Canine Professionals
PO Box 560156
Montverde, FL 34756-0156
(407) 469-2008
iac@mindspring.com
http://www.dogpro.org

The International Association of Canine Professionals (IACP) provides resources for people in all aspects of canine care. It promotes professionalism in all areas of canine care, and communication between members. Regional networking opportunities are offered, as well as educational opportunities for members.

DUDE RANCHER

The Dude Ranchers Association
1122 12th Street
PO Box 2307
Cody, WY 82414
(307) 587 2339
info@duderanch.org
http://www.duderanch.org

The Dude Ranchers Association represents dude ranchers in 12 states and two Canadian provinces. It was formed in 1926 to best represent the interests of dude ranchers, and has grown significantly. Its Web site contains practical, useful information for members and others who are interested in becoming involved in dude ranching. It also is a comprehensive source of information for people interested in vacationing at a dude ranch. The Dude Ranchers Association holds an annual conference, publishes a monthly newsletter, and provides other services for members.

DudeRanches.com
http://www.duderanches.com
Web site featuring lists of dude and guest ranches across North America, along with information on employment, ranch map, ranch specials, dude ranch tips, and much more.

Sprucedale Guest Ranch
PO Box 880
Eagar, AZ 85925
(928) 333-4984
sprucedale@sprucedaleranch.com
http://www.sprucedaleranch.com

Sprucedale Guest Ranch is a family-run dude ranch located in the mountains of Arizona. Its Web site can give you an idea of what a dude ranch looks like and the activities that occur there. It also outlines a daily schedule so that you can get a glimpse of what owning or even staying at a dude ranch is like.

EQUINE DENTIST

The Academy of Equine Dentistry
PO Box 999
Glenns Ferry, ID 83623
(208) 366-2315
academy@equinedentalacademy.com
http://www.equinedentalacademy.com

The Academy of Equine Dentistry is a facility that teaches students the practice of dentistry for horses. It is run by practicing equine dentists and dental technicians who are committed to training others to tend to the important task of caring for the teeth of horses. Courses include the history of equine dentistry, the anatomy of a horse's head and teeth, how horses' teeth are numbered, correct examination techniques, and the basic function of the teeth and how they affect the body of a horse. Courses also address the business aspects of horse dentistry, and students are required to learn the proper use of instruments through hands-on training.

American School of Equine Dentistry
36691 Sawmill Lane
Purcellville, VA 20132
http://www.amscheqdentistry.com

The American School of Equine Dentistry is a private dentistry school that promotes an integrated approach to equine health care.

American Veterinary Dental Society
618 Church Street, Suite 220
Nashville, TN 37219
(800) 332-AVDS
http://www.avds-online.org/

The American Veterinary Dental Society (AVDS) was founded in 1976 to create a forum for advancing the knowledge, education, and awareness of veterinary dentistry among veterinarians, students, and the public. The AVDS includes more than 900 U.S. members, and is the largest organization of veterinary dental professionals in the world. Membership in the AVDS is open to any veterinarian, dentist, hygienist, technician or individual with an interest in veterinary dentistry.

International Association of Equine Dentistry
2436 South I-35 East
Suite 376 – PMB 203
Denton, TX 76205
info@equine.dk
http://www.iaeqd.org

The International Association of Equine Dentistry (IAED) was established to promote the profession of equine dentistry, both among veterinarians and equine dental technicians. It holds an annual conference and provides continuing education opportunities. Its Web site also provides consumer information concerning locating and hiring a reliable horse dentist.

EXOTIC ANIMAL VETERINARIAN

American Association of Wildlife Veterinarians
http://www.aawv.net

This nonprofit association works to enhance the contribution of veterinary medicine to the welfare of the wildlife resource and to encourage and promote a philosophy of animal management and preventative medicine as it relates to free-ranging species. Active membership is open to graduates of colleges or schools of veterinary medicine who support the objectives of the AAWV, and who

work with or have an interest in the application of veterinary medicine to the problems of free-ranging wildlife. Students in college or schools of veterinary medicine who are interested in the objectives of the AAWV may become student members.

American Association of Zoo Veterinarians
6 North Pennell Road
Media, PA 19063
(610) 892-4812
http://www.aazv.org

The American Association of Zoo Veterinarians aims to develop programs for preventive medicine, husbandry, and scientific research in the field of veterinary medicine dealing with captive and free-ranging wild animals. The association also tries to provide a forum for the discussion of problems related to the field of captive and free-ranging wild animals, publish and distribute scientific information, and uphold the professional ethics of zoo veterinary medicine.

American Veterinary Medical Association
1931 North Meacham Road, Suite 100
Schaumburg, IL 60173
(847) 925-8070
avmainfo@avma.org
http://www.avma.org

The American Veterinary Medical Association traces its origins to 1963, when a group of veterinary surgeons met in New York City. Its goal is to advance the art and science of veterinary medicine, and to represent the views of its members to government, pet owners, the media, academia, and agriculture. Association members benefits include journals, educational opportunities, an annual conference, networking opportunities, and more.

Association of Exotic Mammal Veterinarians
PO Box 396
Weare, NH 03281-0396
(603) 529-4980
info@aemv.org
http://www.aemv.org

The Association of Exotic Mammal Veterinarians was founded in 2000 to advance the practice of caring for pets such as ferrets, rabbits, guinea pigs, and rodents. It is an educational support organization for practicing exotic animal veterinarians and students. The association offers continuing education opportunities to members and publishes the Journal of Exotic Mammal Medicine and Surgery.

Association of Avian Veterinarians
PO Box 811720
Boca Raton, FL 33481
http://www.aav.org

Nonprofit organization dedicated to helping avian veterinarians increase their competence and confidence in their knowledge and skills, and helping to educate bird owners about the responsible care of birds.

Association of Primate Veterinarians
9190 Crestwyn Hills Drive
Memphis, TN 38125-8538
(215) 774-9603
http://www.primatevets.org/contact.asp

This nonprofit association was founded to promote the dissemination of information about the health, care, and welfare of nonhuman primates, to provide a way for primate veterinarians to discuss matters regarding nonhuman primates, and to promote fellowship among primate veterinarians.

Association of Reptilian and Amphibian Veterinarians
PO Box 605

Chester Heights, PA 19017
(610) 358-9530
http://www.arav.org

A nonprofit international organization of veterinarians and herpetologists founded in 1991. Its goal is to improve reptilian and amphibian veterinary care and husbandry through education, exchange of ideas, and research. The Association of Reptilian and Amphibian Veterinarians (ARAV) promotes conservation and humane treatment of all reptilian and amphibian species through education, captive breeding, and reptilian and amphibian habitat preservation.

FARRIER

American Farrier's Association
4059 Iron Works Parkway, Suite 1
Lexington, KY 40511
(859) 233-7411
http://www.americanfarriers.org

The American Farrier's Association is North America's organization for men and women who make their living as professional farriers. The AFA began in 1971 in Albuquerque, New Mexico, with a small organization of farriers that wanted to help organize the farrier industry and provide some direction for the future. Ever since, the AFA has continued to grow into an association of international scope that is continuing to provide direction and growth for the industry. Today, the AFA promotes the profession and serves as a representative of farriery interests within the horse world. The AFA actively monitors legislation and showing rules, and acts as an advocate of farriers in relations with veterinarians, breed and sport associations, and state and federal government agencies. Certification, education, research, and communication projects promoted and administered by the AFA are designed to help farriers provide improved service to horses and horseowners.

The Guild of Professional Farriers
2020 Pennsylvania Avenue, NW, Suite #800
Washington, DC 20006
http://www.horseshoes.com/assoc/national/guild/index.htm

The Guild of Professional Farriers was created to define a valid standard of practical competence for professional farriers, and to effectively represent these farriers and the profession. The Guild is a nonprofit organization that does not endorse or support state licensing of farriers or other government interference with the rights of horseowners to make their own decisions regarding the care of their own animals. Guild registration is a voluntary program through which qualified farriers may obtain a formal credential indicating that they meet a meaningful standard of professional competence as determined by technical knowledge and practical skills examinations, length of field experience, and other factors. The minimum qualification for entering the Guild registry is the Registered Journeyman Farrier (RJF) credential.

Oklahoma Horseshoeing School
26446 Horseshoe Circle
Purcell, OK 73080
(800) 538-1383
http://www.horseshoes.com/schools/okschool/contents/contents.htm

The Oklahoma Horseshoeing School was founded in 1973 and trains men and women from all over the world. More than 95 percent of its graduates go on to become employed in the horse industry. Its 16-week professional horseshoeing course is designed to begin at the basic level and develop a student to feel comfortable shoeing horses.

Sisterhood Of Shoers
804 Vann Street
Vidalia, GA 30474

An association for female farriers whose mission is to provide the format and opportunity for female farriers to meet each other and share ideas. They provide the avenues for association, recognition, education, communication, encouragement, product development, business development, insurance, advertisement, and the like.

GOURMET DOG TREAT BAKER

Great Dog Bakery
15365 SW Beaverton Creek Court
Beaverton, OR 97006
(877) 292-1113
info@greatdogbakery.com
http://www.greatdogbakery.com

Web site of dog biscuit chef Daryl Ostrovsky, who creates homemade all-natural dog treats.

Start Your Own Dog Bakery Business
http://www.mymommybiz.com/ebooks/bakeryibm.html

An Internet how-to for those interested in becoming a dog biscuit chef.

Three Dog Bakery
1843 N. Topping Avenue
Kansas City, MO 64120
(800) 487-3287
threedog@threedog.com
http://www.threedog.com

A dog biscuit bakery with lots of extras.

HOLISTIC VETERINARIAN

Academy of Veterinary Homeopathy
PO Box 9280
Wilmington, DE 19809
(866) 652-1590
http://www.theavh.org

Nonprofit academy open to licensed vets and vet students that provides conferences and information to members.

American Academy of Veterinary Acupuncture
100 Roscommon Drive, Suite 320
Middletown, CT 06457
(860) 635-6300
http://www.aava.org

The American Academy of Veterinary Acupuncture (AAVA) is a not-for-profit organization, formed in 1998 in response to the restructuring of the International Veterinary Acupuncture Society (IVAS). The AAVA was formed to meet the specific needs of American veterinary acupuncturists. The AAVA is an affiliate organization, and is fully recognized by IVAS.

American Holistic Veterinary Medical Association
2218 Old Emmorton Road
Bel Air, MD 21015
(410) 569-0795
office@ahvma.org
http://www.ahvma.org

The American Holistic Veterinary Medical Association is an organization whose purpose is to function as a forum for the exploration of alternative and complementary areas of health care in veterinary medicine.

Veterinary Botanical Medicine Association
Bells Ferry Veterinary Hospital
6410 Highway 92
Acworth GA 30102
DrWynn@vbma.org
http://www.vbma.org

The Veterinary Botanical Medicine Association is a group of veterinarians and herbalists dedicated to developing responsible herbal practice by encouraging research and education, strengthening industry relations, keeping herbal tradition alive as a valid information source, and increasing professional acceptance of herbal medicine for animals. The association offers a referral directory of member vets, along with a library of public information, including links, books, an herbal database, and more.

HORSE WHISPERER

Dances With Horses, Inc.
PO Box 819
Rexburg, ID 83440
(800) 871-7635
http://www.horsewhisperer.com

Web site by whisperer Frank Bell, who offers information about his theory, technique, and timing of this remarkable system on this Web site. His methods offer tools for preparing any horse to be ridden, whether a young horse, problem horse, or seasoned campaigner.

Natural Horse People
28 Hill Lawn
Brislington
Bristol BS4 4PH
UK
011-44-7712-893567
http://www.naturalhorsepeople.com

Natural Horse People is an unbiased, friendly, worldwide community supported by resident natural horse experts that offers a place to learn about horsemanship and holistic natural horsekeeping where members can talk directly to a wide range of resident experts.

MARINE MAMMAL TRAINER

DolphinTrainer.com
1370 Trancas Street, #402
Napa, CA 95448
Dolphintrainer01@aol.com
http://www.dolphintrainer.com

DolphinTrainer.com is a Web site dedicated to people who work with marine mammals, and those interested in becoming professional marine mammal trainers. The site contains a wealth of information about marine mammals and careers. It was founded and is maintained by professional marine mammal trainers, and contains recommended reading and links to other, useful sites.

International Association for Aquatic Animal Medicine
http://www.iaaam.org

The International Association for Aquatic Animal Medicine (IAAAM) is an organization of individuals who are professionally interested in and devote a significant amount of time to the practice of aquatic animal medicine, teaching and research in aquatic animal medicine, or the husbandry and management of aquatic animals.

International Marine Animals Trainer Association
1200 South Lakeshore Drive
Chicago, IL 60605
(312) 692-3193
info@IMATA.org
http://www.imata.org

The International Marine Animals Trainer Association (IMATA) was founded with the purpose of promoting cooperation, communication, and professionalism among trainers. It provides opportunities for education for its members and sponsors an annual conference. Its Web site contains information for people interested in becoming professional marine animal trainers.

The Society for Marine Mammalogy
http://www.marinemammalogy.org

The nonprofit Society for Marine Mammalogy was founded at San Francisco in 1981 to evaluate and promote the educational, scientific, and managerial advancement of marine mammal science. The organization also provides information about conserving and managing marine mammal resources.

MUSHER

Alaska Dog Mushers Association
PO Box 70662
Fairbanks, AK 99707-0662
(907) 457-MUSH [6874]
http://www.sleddog.org

The Alaska Dog Mushers Association, Inc., founded in 1948, is a nonprofit organization dedicated to the promotion of the sport of sprint sled dog racing and the proper care, training and treatment of sled dogs. ADMA conducts the annual Open North American Championship, the oldest continuously run dog sled race in the world. ADMA is known for its world-class trails and award-winning races.

Alaska Sled Dog & Racing Association
PO Box 110569
Anchorage, AK 99511
http://www.asdra.org

The Alaska Sled Dog and Racing Association (ASDRA) was formed in 1949 to promote and preserve the Alaskan tradition of dog mushing. ASDRA's volunteers have developed and maintained the dedicated sled-dog trails in Far North Bicentennial Park and the Campbell Tract for 50 years. The nonprofit club puts on internationally recognized races; a junior mushing program provides education and winter recreation for mushers from 4 to 17 years. Members sponsor events sharing their sport with the community and tourists.

Sled Dog Central
2850 275th Street
St. Croix Falls, WI 54024
(715) 488-2434
info@sleddogcentral.com
http://www.sleddogcentral.com

Sled Dog Central is an online organization for mushers and sled dog enthusiasts, providing a wide variety of information, links to other sites, race and event listings, and sources for mushing equipment. Users of the site can exchange information about veterinary issues, shopping tips, upcoming events, clubs and organizations, animal nutrition issues, and more. The site also includes a mentor program that connects experienced mushers with beginners.

International Association of Canine Professionals
PO Box 560156
Montverde, FL 34756-0156
(407) 469-2008
iac@mindspring.com
http://www.dogpro.org

The International Association of Canine Professionals (IACP) provides resources for people in all aspects of canine care. It promotes professionalism in all areas of canine care, and communication between members. Regional networking opportunities are offered, as well as educational opportunities for members.

International Sled Dog Racing Association
http://www.isdra.org/Default.asp?bhcp=1

The International Sled Dog Racing Association (ISDRA) was formed in 1966 as the central governing body of sled-dog competitions. ISDRA has promoted public interest in the sport, encouraged cooperation between race organizations, created and maintained standardized race management procedures, and promoted the highest standards of animal welfare for canine athletes. ISDRA provides products and services to the sled-dog community worldwide, and is comprised of 13 geographical regions, two national federations, many regional clubs, and more than 750 individual members worldwide. ISDRA sanctions 50 to 60 sled dog events each racing season.

PET CEMETERY OWNER

Hartsdale Pet Cemetery
75 North Central Park Avenue
Hartsdale, NY 10530
(800) 375-5234
http://www.petcem.com

America's first pet burial grounds, founded by veterinarian Samuel Johnson in 1896.

International Association of Pet Cemeteries
5055 Route 11
Ellenburg Depot, NY 12935
(518) 594-3000
http://www.iaopc.com

The IAOPCC (International Association of Pet Cemeteries & Crematories) is a not-for-profit organization dedicated to the advancement of pet cemeteries everywhere through public awareness programs. The International Association of Pet Cemeteries was founded in 1971 in West Chicago by Pat Blosser. Member pet cemeteries are expected to maintain the highest business and ethical standards. IAOPCC operates on a budget that is supported only by dues and other contributions from members. IAOPCC has no paid employees; all efforts are completely voluntary.

PET LAWYER

Animal Legal Defense Fund
170 East Cotati Avenue
Cotati, CA 94931
(707) 795-2533
http://www.aldf.org

Founded by attorneys active in shaping the emerging field of animal law, ALDF has pushed for stronger enforcement of anti-cruelty laws and more humane treatment of animals. Today, ALDF's efforts are supported by hundreds of dedicated attorneys and more than 100,000 members. Every day, ALDF works to protect animals by providing free legal assistance to prosecutors handling cruelty cases, maintaining a database of animal abuse crimes across the country, working to strengthen state anti-cruelty statutes, encouraging the federal government to enforce existing animal protection laws, nurturing the future of animal law through Student Animal Legal Defense Fund chapters, educating the public through seminars, workshops, and other outreach efforts, and supporting lawsuits that explore important issues and expand the boundaries of animal law.

Animal Rights and Pet Law at Megalaw.com
http://www.megalaw.com/top/animal.php

Web site maintained by Megalaw offering state-by-state listing of animal anti-cruelty statutes, other animal rights and pet law statutes and regulations (such as hunter harassment statutes, federal animal welfare act, wild and free-roaming horses and burros act), and government animal rights and pet law resources.

Animal Rights Law Project
http://www.animal-law.org

Rutgers was the first law school in the United States to have animal rights law as part of the regular academic curriculum and to award students academic credit not only for classroom work but also for work on actual cases involving animal issues that were litigated by Francione, Charlton, and associated counsel. The course is offered every semester and is now called "Animal Rights: Theory and Practice." The materials on this Web site include selected documents from some of the legal and regulatory actions litigated by Francione and Charlton. These actions involve: the right of a student to object to vivisection or dissection in the classroom, hunting and wildlife issues, hunter "harassment," wild horses, animal sacrifices, and animal care committees. The Web site also offers on-line handbooks concerning freedom of expression and housing issues involving companion animals. In addition, the Web site offers various essays and journal articles on animal rights and animals and the law, and information about books written by Francione and Charlton. Finally, the Web site contains various state and federal laws and regulations.

PET PHOTOGRAPHER

North American Nature Photography Association
10200 West 44th Avenue, Suite 304
Wheat Ridge, CO 80033
(303) 422-8527
info@nanpa.org
http://www.nanpa.org

The North American Nature Photography Association was formed in 1993 to promote the art of photographing animals and nature. With more than 2,500 members, the organization holds an annual summit and trade show, and establishes standards in the field of nature photography.

Professional Photographers of America, Inc.
229 Peachtree Street, NE, Suite 2200
Atlanta, GA 30303
(404) 522-8600
http://www.ppa.com

The Professional Photographers of America, Inc. is the largest organization of professional photographers in the world, boasting more than 14,000 members in 64 countries. Founded in 1880 as a source of education and community for photographers, the organization currently offers business and personal insurance for it members, business discounts, professional recognition, credential programs and advocacy services. Members also receive a twice-monthly e-mailed newsletter.

PET PSYCHIC

American Association of Psychics
http://www.americanassociationof
psychics.com

Psychic network of professional psychics providing psychic readings, contact mediums, intuitives, numerologists, astrologers, metaphysical & holistic suppliers throughout the USA.

Animal Communications Workshops
http://www.animal-communicator.com

Web site discussing private sessions and workshops with Georgina Cyr, who offers guided meditations to send and receive messages from animals telepathically.

Animal Insights
http://www.animalinsights.com

Animal insights was founded by Carole Devereux in dedication to the advancement of animal welfare through the practice of animal communication, holistic healing, and humane education. The Web site offers information on animal communication, consulting, death and dying, and much more. Devereux conducts animal communication workshops, teaches privately, conducts in-person and telephone consultations, and writes extensively.

Global Psychics Pet and Nature Links
http://www.globalpsychics.com/lp/tips/
petlink.htm

Web site dedicated to a list of links and resources relating to animal communication and pet psychics.

PET PSYCHOLOGIST

Association for the Study of Animal Behavior
82A High Street
Sawston
Cambridge CB2 4HJ
UK
asab@grantais.demon.co.uk
http://asab.nottingham.ac.uk

This British Web site offers information and conferences on animal behavior and careers in this field.

Center for the Integrative Study of Animal Behavior
http://www.indiana.edu/~animal/help/
careers.html

Web site listing all kinds of information about animal behavior and careers, including vet schools, programs in animal behavior, books on animal behavior, internships, associations, resources, and much more.

PetPsych.com

http://www.petpsych.com

Web site run by Dr. David Spiegel, D.V.M., an animal behavior consultant who offers reference information, animal behavior facts, online answers to questions, and much more.

PET SITTER

Happy Paws Pet Sitting
Sue Belford
Douglassville, PA
(610) 385-9767
http://www.happypawspetsittingpa.com

A professional pet-sitting service providing experienced and loving care for pets in the comfort and familiarity of their own home on a daily, weekly, or occasional basis. Happy Paws is an in-your-home, pet-sitting service providing professional, dependable, and loving care for all pets. Sitters with this service are competent, safety conscious, knowledgeable, and compassionate.

Pet Sitters International
201 East King Street
King, NC 27021-9161
(336) 983-9222
http://www.petsit.com/

The largest and most progressive organization for professional pet sitters in the world, PSI is a membership association that exists to provide support and services to its members. It was founded in 1994 in order to support professional pet sitters through superior customer service, excellent benefits and educational tools to help them succeed in achieving their career goals of excellence in pet sitting. Pet Sitters International is a for-profit corporation that serves the needs of its for-profit member businesses. It is organized to educate professional pet sitters and to

promote, support, and recognize excellence in pet sitting. PSI membership benefits include group rates on liability insurance and dishonesty bonds, client referrals, Web page design and hosting and discounts on other business services.

National Association of Professional Pet Sitters
15000 Commerce Parkway, Suite C
Mt. Laurel, NJ 08054
(856) 439-0324
napps@ahint.com
http://www.purrfectpetsitting.net

The National Association of Professional Pet Sitters provides education, networking, and professional integrity, helping foster success. The National Association of Professional Pet Sitters is a nonprofit membership organization originally founded in 1989, to promote excellence among pet sitters and to serve as a voice for the expanding industry. NAPPS provides educational tools to its membership, along with a certification program that assists in the development of pet care as well as business skills.

PETTING ZOO OPERATOR

American Zoo and Aquarium Association
8403 Colesville Road, Suite 710
Silver Spring, MD 20910
(301) 562-0777
http://www.aza.org

The American Zoo and Aquarium Association (AZA) is a nonprofit organization dedicated to the advancement of zoos and aquarium facilities. It works in the areas of conservation, science, education, and recreation. Founded in 1924, the AZA is managed by a board of directors and has more than 5,500 members. It is the largest zoo and aquarium organization in the world.

The National FFA Organization
PO Box 68960
6060 FFA Drive
Indianapolis, IN 46268
(317) 802-6060

The National FFA Organization was founded in 1928 in Kansas City as the Future Farmers of America. Its name was changed in 1998 to better reflect the widening field of agriculture and animal care. The organization is governed by a board of directors and has a board of student officers. Student members belong to chapters organized on a local level, and can participate in state, regional, and national events, as well. The organization provides scholarships to students who qualify.

PET WASTE REMOVAL SPECIALIST

DoodyCalls
5 Burke Court
Palmyra, VA 22963
(800) DoodyCalls [366-3922]
http://www.DoodyCalls.com

Successful pet waste removal company with franchises in four states, founded by Jacob and Susan D'Aniello.

National Association for the Self-Employed
(800) 232-6273
http://www.nase.org

The National Association for the Self-Employed (NASE) is the nation's leading resource for the self-employed and microbusinesses (up to 10 employees), providing a broad range of benefits and support to help the smallest businesses succeed. NASE was founded in 1981 by a group of small-business owners in search of a structure of day-to-day support, benefits, and consolidated buying power that traditionally had been available only to large corporations. Today, the

NASE represents hundreds of thousands of entrepreneurs and micro-businesses, and is the largest nonprofit, nonpartisan association of its kind in the United States.

SHEEP SHEARER

American Sheep Industry Association
9785 Maroon Circle, Suite 360
Centennial, CO 80112
(303) 771-3500
info@sheepusa.org
http://www.sheepusa.org

The American Sheep Industry Association (ASIA) is a national organization representing more than 64,000 people who work in the sheep industry. Founded in 1865 as the National Wool Growers Association, it works to promote legislation favorable to the industry, and works on issues relating to animal health, resource management issues, and science and technology relating to the production of sheep.

Mid-States Wool Growers Cooperative Association
9449 Basil-Western Road NW Canal
Winchester, OH 43110
(800) 841-9665 for states east of the Mississippi
(800) 835-9665 for states west of the Mississippi
http://www.midstateswoolgrowers.com

Web site offering books, magazines, all types of shears and clippers, shearing equipment, and videos about shearing techniques, shearing moccasins, wool bags, and much more.

WILDLIFE REHABILITATOR

National Wildlife Rehabilitators Association
2625 Clearwater Road, Suite 110
St. Cloud, MN 56301

(320) 230-9920
nwra@nwra.org
http://www.nwra.org

The National Wildlife Rehabilitators Association (NWRA) was founded to promote the profession of wildlife rehabilitation, and to contribute to ongoing improvement in the profession through education and standards. Members of the NWRA treat hundreds of thousands of birds and animals each year. Members receive a directory, wildlife rehabilitation journal, and a newsletter. They also are eligible to attend the NWRA's annual symposium.

Orphaned Wildlife Rehabilitation Society (OWL)
3800 72nd Street
Delta, BC
V4K 3N2
Canada
(604) 946-3171
http://www.owlcanada.ca

The Orphaned Wildlife Rehabilitation Society is a nonprofit organization whose volunteers are dedicated to public education and the rehabilitation and release of injured and orphaned birds. Founded in 1985, OWL cares for and rehabilitates injured and orphaned birds of prey (eagles, falcons, hawks, osprey, and owls), and offers educational activities about wildlife and environmental concerns. It offers an on-site school program and outreach program and works with cooperative education programs, welfare incentive programs, and clients with a mental health or cognitive disability.

The Wildlife Rehabilitation Information Directory
http://www.tc.umn.edu/~devo0028

The source on the Web for information on wildlife rehabilitation. Here you will find information on what to do with injured wildlife and who to contact. Information is provided for the public and for the professional wildlife rehabilitator. Many links are provided to sites of interest relating to the field. Information is also present about wildlife in general.

Wildlife Rescue and Rehabilitation
PO Box 369
Kendalia, TX 78027
(830) 336-2725
Info@wildlife-rescue.org
http://www.wildlife-rescue.org

Wildlife Rescue and Rehabilitation, Inc. is a nonprofit organization dedicated to rescuing, rehabilitating, and releasing wildlife that has been injured, orphaned, or displaced. Some animals are given permanent care and shelter, when applicable. The agency, which is an accredited sanctuary, was started in 1977 by Lynn Cuny, who still directs the organization. It maintains a 24-hour hotline on which people can report animals that need help. In addition to a paid staff, the organization relies on hundreds of trained volunteers who respond to calls and help with other tasks.

World Wildlife Fund
1250 24th Street, NW
Washington, DC 20037
(202) 293-4800
info@worldwildlife.org
http://www.worldwildlife.org

The World Wildlife Fund was founded in 1960 by Sir Julian Huxley, a well known biologist who was deeply disturbed by wildlife and environmental destruction he witnessed during a trip to Africa. The organization is the largest, privately funded international conservation agency in the world, with more than 30 countries participating.

Membership in the World Wildlife Fund stands at more than 5 million people. The organization primarily works to protect endangered species and their habitats.

ZOOKEEPER

American Association of Zookeepers, Inc.
3601 Southwest 29th Street, Suite 133
Topeka, KS 66614
aazkoffice@zk.kscoxmail.com
http://www.aazk.org

The American Association of Zookeepers, Inc. (AAZK) is a nonprofit organization for professional zookeepers and others interested in animal care and conservation. Founded in 1967 in San Diego, its intent is to encourage a professional approach to animal care and professionalism amongst members. The organization, which has about 2,800 members, provides an online forum for members to share information and concerns, publications, and regional meetings and conferences.

American Zoo and Aquarium Association
8403 Colesville Road, Suite 710
Silver Spring, MD 20910
(301) 562-0777
http://www.aza.org

The American Zoo and Aquarium Association (AZA) is a nonprofit organization dedicated to the advancement of zoos and aquarium facilities. It works in the areas of conservation, science, education, and recreation. Founded in 1924, the AZA is managed by a board of directors and has more than 5,500 members. It is the largest zoo and aquarium organization in the world.

Association of British Wild Animal Keepers
http://www.abwak.co.uk

The objectives of this association are to improve cooperation among international zookeepers, to organize meetings and conventions, to improve the professional competence of everyone involved with wild animal husbandry, and to support the conservation of wildlife throughout the world.

Elephant Managers Association
http://www.elephant-managers.com

The EMA is about elephants, conservation, and education. Whether it's issues that surround elephants in zoos or the threats elephants face in the wild, the EMA is striving to conserve these animals. EMA members are elephant professionals from around the world—researchers, curators, veterinarians, and handlers—all working with more than 25 member institutions to ensure elephants' survival. EMA members are also people who care about elephants—people who know how important elephants are, want to learn more about them, and wish to support the EMA's conservation efforts

International Zoo Educators Association
http://www.izea.net

The International Zoo Educators Association is dedicated to expanding the educational impact of zoos and aquariums worldwide. Its dual mission is to improve zoo education programs and provide members with access to the latest thinking, techniques, and information in conservation education.

APPENDIX B. ONLINE CAREER RESOURCES

This volume offers a look inside a wide range of unusual and unique careers that might appeal to someone interested in working with animals. Although this book highlights general information about each job, it can really only give you a glimpse into these careers. These entries are intended to whet your appetite and provide you with some career options you never knew existed.

Before jumping into any career, you'll want to do more research to make sure that it's really something you want to pursue for the rest of your life. You'll want to learn as much as you can about the careers in which you're interested; that way, as you continue to do research and talk to people in those particular fields, you can ask informed and intelligent questions that will help you make your decisions.

You might want to research the education options for learning the skills you'll need to be successful, along with scholarships, work-study programs, and other opportunities to help you finance that education.

✳ **A word about Internet safety:** The Internet is a wonderful resource for networking. Many job and career sites have forums where students can interact with other people interested in and working in that field. Some sites even offer online chats where people can communicate with each other in real time. They provide students and jobseekers opportunities to make connections and maybe even begin to lay the groundwork for future employment. But as you use these forums and chats remember, anyone could be on the other side of that computer screen, telling you exactly what you want to hear. It's easy to get wrapped up in the excitement of the moment when you are on a forum or in a chat, interacting with people that share your career interests and aspirations. But be cautious about what kind of personal information you make available on the forums and in the chats; never give out your full name, address, or phone number. And never agree to meet with someone that you have met online.

SEARCH ENGINES

When looking for information, there are lots of search engines that will help you to find out more about these jobs along with others that might interest you. And while you might already have a favorite search engine, you might want to take some time to check out some of the others that are out there. Some have features that might help you find information not located with the others. Several engines will offer suggestions for ways to narrow your results, or related phrases you might want to search along with your search results. This is handy if you are having trouble locating exactly what you want.

Another good thing to do is to learn how to use the advanced search features of your favorite search engines. Knowing that might help you to zero-in on exactly the information for which you are searching without wasting time looking through pages of irrelevant hits.

As you use the Internet to search information on the perfect career, keep in mind that like anything you find on the Internet, you need to consider the source from which the information comes.

Some of the most popular Internet search engines are:

AllSearchEngines.com
www.allsearchengines.com
This search engine index has links to the major search engines along with search engines grouped by topic. The site includes a page with more than 75 career and job search engines at http://www. allsearchengines.com/careerjobs.html.

AlltheWeb
http://www.alltheweb.com

AltaVista
http://www.altavista.com

Ask.com
http://www.ask.com

Dogpile
http://www.dogpile.com

Excite
http://www.excite.com

Google
http://www.google.com

HotBot
http://www.hotbot.com

LookSmart
http://www.looksmart.com

Lycos
http://www.lycos.com

Mamma.com
http://www.mamma.com

MSN Network
http://www.msn.com

My Way
http://www.goto.com

Teoma
http://www.directhit.com

Vivisimo
http://www.vivisimo.com

Yahoo!
http://www.yahoo.com

HELPFUL WEB SITES

The Internet is a wealth of information on careers—everything from the mundane to the outrageous. There are thousands of sites devoted to helping you find the perfect job for your interests, skills, and talents. The sites listed here are some of the most helpful ones that the authors came across and/or used while researching the jobs in this volume. The sites are listed in alphabetical order. They are offered for your information, and are not endorsed by the authors.

All Experts
http://www.allexperts.com
"The oldest & largest free Q&A service on the Internet," AllExperts.com has thousands of volunteer experts to answer your questions. You can also read replies to questions asked by other people. Each expert has an online profile to help you pick someone who might be best suited to answer your question. Very easy to use, it's a great resource for finding experts who can help to answer your questions.

America's Career InfoNet
http://www.acinet.org
A wealth of information! You can get a feel for the general job market; check out wages and trends in a particular state for

different jobs; and learn more about the knowledge, skills, abilities, and tasks for specific careers; and learn about required certifications and how to get them. You can search over 5,000 scholarship and other financial opportunities to help you further your education. A huge career resources library has links to nearly 6,500 online resources. And for fun, you can take a break and watch one of nearly 450 videos featuring real people at work; everything from custom tailors to engravers, glassblowers to silversmiths.

Animal Jobs
http://www.animaljobs.com

A Web site dedicated to all kinds of animal jobs, which posts open positions, the ability to post your resume, animal-related company profiles, and related job sites.

Ark Animals: Unusual Animal Careers
http://www.arkanimals.com/Career/Career1.html

Ark Animals is an online magazine dedicated to the topics of domestic pets, exotic animals, and captive wildlife. Topics include animal behavior, animal training, enrichment, and related issues such as conservation, education, and research. You'll also find a pet behavior and pet training section, lists of animal books, safari opportunities, and a very popular unusual animal career series.

Backdoor Jobs
http://www.backdoorjobs.com

This is the Web site of the popular book by the same name, now in its third edition. While not as extensive as the book, the site still offers a wealth of information for people looking for short-term opportunities: internships, seasonal jobs, volunteer vacations, and work abroad situations. Job opportunities

are classified into several categories: Adventure Jobs, Camps, Ranches & Resort Jobs, Ski Resort Jobs, Jobs in the Great Outdoors, Nature Lover Jobs, Sustainable Living and Farming Work, Artistic & Learning Adventures, Heart Work, and Opportunities Abroad.

Boston Works—Job Explainer
http://bostonworks.boston.com/globe/job_explainer/archive.html

For nearly 18 months, the Boston Globe ran a weekly series profiling a wide range of careers. Some of the jobs were more traditional. Others were very unique and unusual. The profiles discuss an "average" day, challenges of the job, required training, salary, and more. Each profile gives an up close, personal look at that particular career. In addition, The Boston Works Web site (http://bostonworks.boston.com) has a lot of good, general employment-related information.

Career Guide to Industries
http://www.bls.gov/oco/cg/cgindex.htm

For someone interested in working in a specific industry, but who may be undecided about exactly what career to pursue, this site is the place to start. Put together by the U.S. Department of Labor, you can learn more about the industry, working conditions, employment, occupations (in the industry), training and advancement, earnings, outlook, and sources of additional information.

Career Planning at About.com
http://careerplanning.about.com

Like most of the other About.com topics, the career planning area is a wealth of information, and links to other information on the Web. Among the excellent essentials are career planning A-to-Z, a career planning glossary, information on career choices, and a free career planning class. There are many great articles and other excellent resources.

Career Prospects in Virginia

http://www3.ccps.virginia.edu/career_prospects/default-search.html

Career Prospects is a database of entries with information about over 400 careers. Developed by the Virginia Career Resource Network, the online career information resource of the Virginia Department of Education, Office of Career and Technical Education Services, this database was intended as a source of information about jobs "important to Virginia," but it's actually a great source of information for anyone. While some of the information such as wages, outlook, and some of the requirements may apply only to Virginia, the other information for each job, like what's it like, getting ahead, skills, and the links will be of help to anyone interested in that career.

Career Voyages

http://www.careervoyages.gov

"The ultimate road trip to career success," sponsored by the U.S. Department of Labor and the U.S. Department of Education. This site features sections for students, parents, career changers, and career advisors with information and resources aimed to that specific group. The FAQ offers great information about getting started, the high-growth industries, how to find your perfect job, how to make sure you're qualified for the job you want, tips for paying for the training and education you need, and more. Also interesting are the hot careers and the emerging fields.

Dream Jobs

http://www.salary.com/careers/
layouthtmls/crel_display_Cat10.html

The staff at Salary.com takes a look at some wild, wacky, outrageous, and totally cool ways to earn a living. The jobs they highlight include pro skateboarder, computer game guru, nose, diplomat, and much more. The profiles don't offer links or resources for more information, but they are informative and fun to read.

FabJob—Career Guides and Job Advice

http://www.fabjob.com

Dreaming of making it big in an absolutely fabulous career like a pop star, cartoonist, personal trainer, or video game developer? Then the FabJob guides might be your ticket to success. There are currently over 60 full-length titles in the series, with more in the works. Each book covers everything you need to know to be successful in the job of your dreams. The titles range in price from about $14.95 to about $34.95. You can get a good feel for the information contained in each of the books at the Web site. And, each of the books comes with a money-back guarantee. In addition to offering the career guides, the "fabadvice" section has dozens of great articles for those hoping to pursue their dreams.

Find It! in DOL

http://www.dol.gov/dol/findit.htm

A handy source for finding information at the extensive U.S. Department of Labor Web site. You can "Find It!" by broad topic category, or by audience, which includes a section for students.

Fine Living: *Radical Sabbatical*

http://www.fineliving.com/fine/episode_archive/0,1663,FINE_1413_14,00.html#Series873

The show Radical Sabbatical *on the Fine Living network looks at people willing to take a chance and follow their dreams and passions. The show focuses on individuals between the ages of 20 and 65 who have made the decision to leave successful, lucrative careers to start over, usually in an unconventional career. You can read all about these people and their journeys on the show's Web site.*

Free Salary Survey Reports and Cost-of-Living Reports
http://www.salaryexpert.com

Based on information from a number of sources, Salary Expert will tell you what kind of salary you can expect to make for a certain job in a certain geographic location. Salary Expert has information on hundreds of jobs; everything from your more traditional white- and blue-collar jobs, to some unique and out of the ordinary professions like acupressurist, blacksmith, denture waxer, taxidermist, and many others. With sections covering schools, crime, community comparison, community explorer, and more, the moving center is a useful area for people who need to relocate for training or employment.

Fun Jobs
http://www.funjobs.com

Fun Jobs has job listings for adventure, outdoor, and fun jobs at ranches, camps, ski resorts, and more. The job postings have a lot of information about the position, requirements, benefits, and responsibilities so that you know what you are getting into ahead of time. And, you can apply online for most of the positions. The Fun Companies link will let you look up companies in an A-to-Z listing, or you can search for companies in a specific area or by keyword. The company listings offer you more detailed information about the location, types of jobs available, employment qualifications, and more.

Get That Gig
http://www.getthatgig.com

Looking for a really cool job? This is the place to be. Arranged by category, you can select the area that interests you the most: Art & Design, Entertainment, Law & Public Safety, Sales & Marketing, Sports & Fitness, and more than a dozen others. Once inside the category of your choice, you can check out jobs and internships, interviews with people who already have a great gig in that area, cool company of the month, related links and more. You can chat with others looking for their great gig on the "Gig Gab" forums. And, on a more practical note, you can search for jobs and post your resume.

Girls Can Do
http://www.girlscando.com

"Helping Girls Discover Their Life's Passions," Girls Can Do has opportunities, resources, and a lot of other cool stuff for girls ages 8 to 18. Girls can explore sections on Outdoor Adventure, Sports, My Body, The Arts, Sci-Tech, Change the World, and Learn, Earn, and Intern. In addition to reading about women in all sorts of careers, girls can explore a wide range of opportunities and information that will help them grow into strong, intelligent, capable women.

Great Web Sites for Kids
http://www.ala.org/gwstemplate.cfm?section=greatwebsites&template=/cfapps/gws/default.cfm

Great Web Sites for Kids is a collection of more than 700 sites organized into a variety of categories, including animals, sciences, the arts, reference, social sciences, and more. All of the sites included here have been approved by a committee made up of professional librarians and educators. You can even submit your favorite great site for possible inclusion.

Hot Jobs—Career Tools Home
http://www.hotjobs.com/htdocs/tools/index-us.html

While the jobs listed at Hot Jobs are more on the traditional side, the Career Tools area has a lot of great resources for anyone looking for a job. You'll find information about how to write a resume and a cover letter, how to put together a career portfolio, interviewing tips, links to career assessments, and much more.

Job Descriptions & Job Details
http://www.job-descriptions.org

Search for descriptions and details for more than 13,000 jobs at this site. You can search for jobs by category or by industry. You'd probably be hard pressed to find a job that isn't listed here, and you'll probably find lots of jobs you never imagined existed. The descriptions and details are short, but it's interesting and fun, and might lead you to the career of your dreams.

Job Hunter's Bible
http://www.jobhuntersbible.com

This site is the official online supplement to the book, What Color is Your Parachute? A Practical Manual for Job-Hunters and Career-Changers, *and is a great source of information with lots of informative, helpful articles and links to many more resources.*

Job Profiles
http://www.jobprofiles.org

A collection of profiles where experienced workers share rewards of their job; stressful parts of the job; basic skills the job demands; challenges of the future; and advice on entering the field. The careers include everything from baseball ticket manager to pastry chef and much, much more. The hundreds of profiles are arranged by broad category. While most of the profiles are easy to read, you can checkout the How to browse JobProfiles. org section (http://www.jobprofiles.org/jphowto.htm) if you have any problems.

JobStar
http://www.jobstar.org

Originally founded to serve the residents of northern California, JobStar now serves the nation with a searchable database with more than 30,000 mid- to senior-level jobs as well as resources for Asia and Europe. Topics cover how to get ready for a job search, how to get a resume ready, career guides, and salary info. Unique sections discuss the "hidden job market" (great jobs that are never advertised) as well as how to research the company before you even send in your application.

Major Job Web Sites at Careers.org
http://www.careers.org/topic/01_jobs_10.html

This page at the Careers.org Web site has links for more than 40 of the Web's major job-related Web sites. While you're there, check out the numerous links to additional information.

Monster Jobs
http://www.monster.com

Monster.com is one of the largest, and probably best-known, job resource sites on the Web. It's really one-stop shopping for almost anything job-related that you can imagine. You can find a new job, network, update your resume, improve your skills, plan a job change or relocation, and so much more. Of special interest are the Monster: Cool Careers (http://change. monster.com/archives/coolcareers) and the Monster: Job Profiles (http:// jobprofiles.monster.com) pages, where you can read about some really neat careers. The short profiles also include links to additional information. The Monster: Career Advice *section (http:// content.monster.com/) has resume and interviewing advice, message boards where you can network, relocation tools and advice, and more.*

National Association for Humane and Environmental Education
The Humane Society of the United States
http://www.nahee.org/careers_banner.asp

Founded in 1973, the National Association for Humane and Environmental Education (NAHEE) serves as the youth education affiliate of The Humane Society of the United States (HSUS), and includes information about careers with animals. NAHEE is a nonprofit organization whose work is supported by its Adopt-a-Classroom program, private grants, charitable donations, and allocations from The HSUS.

Occupational Outlook Handbook
http://www.bls.gov/oco

Published by the U.S. Department of Labor's Bureau of Labor Statistics, the Occupational Outlook Handbook *(sometimes referred to as the* OOH*) is the premiere source of career information. The book is updated every two years, so you can be assured that the information you are using to help make your decisions is current. The online version is very easy to use; you can search for a specific occupation, browse though a group of related occupations, or look through an alphabetical listing of all the jobs included in the volume. Each of the entries will highlight the general nature of the job, working conditions, training and other qualifications, job outlook, average earning, related occupations,* and sources of additional information. Each entry covers several pages and is a terrific source to get some great information about a huge variety of jobs.

The Riley Guide: Employment Opportunities and Job Resources on the Internet
http://www.rileyguide.com

The Riley Guide is an amazing collection of job and career resources. Unless you are looking for something specific, one of the best ways to maneuver around the site is with the A-to-Z Index. You can find everything from links to careers in enology to information about researching companies and employers. The Riley Guide is a great place to find just about anything you might be looking for, and probably lots of things you aren't looking for. But be forewarned, it's easy to get lost in the A-to-Z Index, reading about all sorts of interesting things.

USA TODAY Career Focus
http://www.usatoday.com/careers/dream/dreamarc.htm

Several years ago, USA TODAY *ran a series featuring people working in their dream jobs. In the profiles, people discuss how they got their dream job, what they enjoy the most about it, they talk about an average day, their education backgrounds, sacrifices they had to make for their jobs, and more. They also share words of advice for anyone hoping to follow in their footsteps. Most of the articles also feature links where you can find more information. The USATODAY.Com Job Center (http://www.usatoday.com/ money/jobcenter/front.htm) also has links to lots of resources and additional information.*

CAREER TESTS AND INVENTORIES

If you have no idea what career is right for you, there are many resources available online that will help assess your interests and maybe steer you in the right direction. While some of the assessments charge a fee, there are many out there that are free. You can locate more tests and inventories by searching online for "career tests," "career inventories," or "personality inventories." Some of the most popular assessments available online are:

Campbell Interest and Skill Survey (CISS)
http://www.usnews.com/usnews/edu/careers/ccciss.htm

Career Explorer
http://careerexplorer.net/aptitude.asp

Career Focus 2000 Interest Inventory
http://www.iccweb.com/careerfocus

The Career Interests Game
http://career.missouri.edu/students/explore/thecareerinterestsgame.php

The Career Key
http://www.careerkey.org

CAREERLINK Inventory
http://www.mpc.edu/cl/cl.htm

Career Maze
http://www.careermaze.com/home.asp?licensee=CareerMaze

Career Tests at CareerPlanner.com
http://www.careerplanner.com

FOCUS
http://www.focuscareer.com

Keirsey Temperament Test
http://www.keirsey.com

Motivational Appraisal of Personal Potential (MAPP)
http://www.assessment.com

Myers-Briggs Personality Type
http://www.personalitypathways.com/type_inventory.html

Princeton Review Career Quiz
http://www.princetonreview.com/cte/quiz/default.asp

Skills Profiler
http://www.acinet.org/acinet/skills_home.asp

READ MORE ABOUT IT

The following sources and books may help you learn more about careers with animals.

GENERAL CAREERS

Culbreath, Alice N., and Saundra K. Neal. *Testing the Waters: A Teen's Guide to Career Exploration.* New York: JRC Consulting, 1999.

Farr, Michael, LaVerne L. Ludden, and Laurence Shatkin. *200 Best Jobs for College Graduates.* Indianapolis, Ind.: Jist Publishing, 2003.

Fogg, Neeta, Paul Harrington, and Thomas Harrington. *College Majors Handbook with Real Career Paths and Payoffs: The Actual Jobs, Earnings, and Trends for Graduates of 60 College Majors.* Indianapolis, Ind.: Jist Publishing, 2004.

Krannich, Ronald L., and Caryl Rae Krannich. *The Best Jobs for the 1990s and into the 21st Century.* Manassas Park, Va.: Impact Publications, 1995.

Lee, Mary Price, and Richard Lee. *Opportunities in Animal and Pet Care Careers.* New York: McGraw-Hill, 2001.

Mannion, James. *The Everything Alternative Careers Book: Leave the Office Behind and Embark on a New Adventure.* Boston: Adams, 2004.

Maynard, Thane. *Working With Wildlife: A Guide to Careers in the Animal World.* London: Franklin Watts, 1999.

Miller, Louise. *Careers for Animal Lovers & Other Zoological Types.* New York: McGraw-Hill, 2000.

Pasternak, Ceel, and Linda Thornburg. *Cool Careers for Girls With Animals.* Manassas Park, Va.: Impact Publications, 1999.

Pavia, Audrey. *Careers with Animals.* Hauppauge, N.Y.: Barron's Educational Series, 2001.

Reeves, Diane Lindsey. *Career Ideas for Kids Who Like Animals and Nature.* New York: Facts on File, 2000.

Salzberg, Kathy. *How to Start a Home-Based Pet Care Business.* Guilford, Conn.: Globe-Pequot, 2002.

Shenk, Ellen. *Careers With Animals: Exploring Occupations Involving Dogs, Horses, Cats, Birds, Wildlife, And Exotics.* Mechanicsburg, Pa.: Stackpole Books, 2005.

U.S. Bureau of Labor Statistics. *Occupational Outlook Handbook, 2006–07.* Available online at http://stats.bls.gov/oco/home.htm.

ANIMAL BEHAVIORIST

Hanna, Jack. *Monkeys on the Interstate: And Other Tales from America's Favorite Zookeeper.* New York: Doubleday, 1989.

Burby, Liza N. *Jane Goodall: Leading Animal Behaviorist.* New York: PowerKids Press, 1997.

McCarthy, Susan. *Becoming a Tiger: How Baby Animals Learn to Live in the Wild.* New York: HarperCollins, 2004.

ANIMAL FORENSIC SPECIALIST

Camenson, Blythe. *Opportunities in Forensic Careers.* New York: McGraw Hill, 2001.

Jackson, Donna. *Wildlife Detectives: How Forensic Scientists Fight Crimes against Nature*. Boston: Houghton Mifflin, 2002.

ANIMAL SHELTER DIRECTOR

Hess, Elizabeth. *Lost and Found: Dogs, Cats, and Everyday Heroes at a Country Animal Shelter*. Orlando: Harvest Books, 2000.

Leigh, Diane, and Marilee Geyer. *One at a Time: A Week in an American Animal Shelter*. Santa Cruz, Calif.: No Voice Unheard, 2003.

ANIMAL WRANGLER

Beck, Ken, and Jim Clark. *The Encyclopedia Of TV Pets: A Complete History Of Television's Greatest Animal Stars*. Nashville: Rutledge Hill Press, 2002.

Dibra, Bash, and Elizabeth Randolph. *Dog Training by Bash: The Tried and True Techniques of the Dog Trainer to the Stars*. New York: Signet, 1992.

AQUARIST

Hargreaves, Vincent B. *The Complete Book of the Marine Aquarium*. San Diego: Thunder Bay Press, 2002.

Lambert, Derek, and Pat Lambert. *Platies and Swordtails: An Aquarist's Handbook*. London: Blandford Press, 1996.

ASSISTANCE DOG TRAINER

Osborn, Kevin. *A Day in the Life of a Seeing Eye Dog Trainer*. New York: Troll Communications, 1991.

Swanbeck, Steve. *The Seeing Eye*. Charleston, S.C.: Arcadia Publishing, 2002.

DOG DAY CARE OWNER

Moore, Arden. *Doggy Daycare*. Irvine, Calif.: BowTie Press, 2005.

Salzberg, Kathy. *How to Start a Home-Based Pet Care Business*. Guilford, Conn.: Globe Pequot, 2002.

DOG GROOMER

Gleeson, Eileen. *Ultimate Dog Grooming*. Buffalo, N.Y.: Firefly Books, 2003.

Ogle, Madeline Bright. *From Problems to Profits: The Madson Management System for Pet Grooming Businesses*. Sonora, Calif.: The Madson Group, 1997.

T.F.H. Publications. *All 87 Breed Dog Grooming for the Beginner*. Neptune City, N.J.: T.F.H. Publications, 1995.

DOG HANDLER

Alston, George. *The Winning Edge: Show Ring Secrets*. New York: Howell Book House, Inc., 1992.

Coile, D. Caroline. *Show Me!: A Dog Showing Primer*. Hauppauge, N.Y.: Barrons Educational Series, 1997.

Green, Peter, and Mario Migliorini. *New Secrets of Successful Show Dog Handling*. New York: Time Warner, 2001.

DOG SHOW JUDGE

Caras, Roger A. *Going for the Blue: Inside the World of Show Dogs and Dog Shows*. New York: Warner, 1992.

Cole, Robert W. *An Eye for a Dog: Illustrated Guide to Judging Purebred Dogs*. Wenatchee, Wash.: Dogwise Publishing, 2004.

DUDE RANCHER

Gleason, Alice. *Starting From Scratch: The Adventures of a Lady Dude Rancher*.

Choteau, Mont.: Star Route Publishing, 2000.

Stoecklein, David R. *Dude Ranches of the American West*. Ketchum, Idaho: Stoecklein Publishing, 2004.

EQUINE DENTIST

Baker, Gordon. *Equine Dentistry*. London: W.B. Saunders Company, 2004.

Jeffrey, Dale. *Horse Dentistry: The Theory and Practice Of Equine Dental Maintenence*. Glenns Ferry, Idaho: World Wide Equine, 1996.

EXOTIC ANIMAL VETERINARIAN

Ballard, Bonnie. *Exotic Animal Medicine for the Veterinary Technician*. Ames, Iowa: Iowa State Press, 2003.

Thomas, Tully. *A Technician's Guide to Exotic Animal Care: A Guide for Veterinary Technicians*. Lakewood, Colo.: American Animal Hospital Association, 2001.

FARRIER

Baskins, Don. *Well-Shod: A Horseshoeing Guide for Owners & Farriers*. Colorado Springs, Colo.: Western Horseman, 2004.

Lungwitz, Anton. *A Textbook of Horseshoeing for Horseshoers and Veterinarians*. Corvallis, Ore.: Oregon State University Press, 1995.

Wiseman, Robert F. *The Complete Horse-shoeing Guide*. 2nd ed. Norman, Okla.: University of Oklahoma Press, 1995.

GOURMET DOG TREAT BAKER

Dye, Dan, and Mark Beckloff. *Three Dog Bakery Cookbook*. Kansas City, Mo.: Salamander Books, Ltd., 2001.

———. *Short Tails and Treats from the Three Dog Bakery*. Kansas City, Mo.: Salamander Books, Ltd., 1996.

Lee, Mary Price, and Richard Lee. *Opportunities in Animal and Pet Care Careers*. New York: McGraw-Hill, 2001.

HOLISTIC VETERINARIAN

Goldstein, Martin, D.V.M. *The Nature of Animal Healing: The Definitive Holistic Medicine Guide to Caring for Your Dog and Cat*. New York: Ballantine, 2000.

Maze, Stephanie. *I Want to Be a Veterinarian*. New York: Harcourt, 1999.

Zucker, Martin. *Veterinarians' Guide to Natural Remedies for Dogs: Safe and Effective Alternative Treatments and Healing Techniques from the Nation's Top Holistic Veterinarians*. New York: Three Rivers Press, 1999.

HORSE WHISPERER

Ainslee, Tom, and Bonnie Ledbetter. *The Body Language of Horses: Revealing the Nature of Equine Needs, Wishes and Emotions and How Horses Communicate Them*. New York: William Morrow, 1980.

Bell, Frank, and Sylvia Scott. *Gentle Solutions: Frank Bell's Seven Steps To A Safer Horse*. Rexburg, Idaho: Dances With Horses Inc., 2002.

Roberts, Monty. *The Man Who Listens to Horses*. New York: Ballantine Books, 1998.

———. *Horse Sense for People*. New York: Penguin, 2002.

MARINE MAMMAL TRAINER

Blanchard, Kenneth. *Whale Done!: The Power of Positive Relationships*. New York: Free Press, 2002.

Samansky, Terry S. *Starting Your Career as a Marine Mammal Trainer*. 2nd ed. DolphinTrainer.com, 2002.

MUSHER

Bowers, Dan. *Back of the Pack: An Iditarod Rookie Musher's Alaska Pilgrimage to Nome*. Anchorage, Alaska: Publication Consultants, 1996.

Brown, Tricia. *Lessons My Sled Dog Taught Me: Humor and Heartwarming Tails from Alaska's Mushers*. Seattle: Epicenter Press, 1998.

PET CEMETERY OWNER

Lanci-Altomare, Michelle. *Good-Bye My Friend: Pet Cemeteries, Memorials, and Other Ways to Remember*. Irvine, Calif.: BowTie Press, 2000.

Martin, Edward C. *Dr. Johnson's Apple Orchard: The Story of America's First Pet Cemetery*. Hartsdale, N.Y.: Hartsdale Canine Cemetery, 1997.

PET LAWYER

Congalton, David, and Charlotte Alexander. *When Your Pet Outlives You: Protecting Animal Companions After You Die*. Troutdale, Ore.: New Sage Press, 2002.

Waisman, Sonia A., Bruce A. Wagman, and Pamela D. Frasch. *Animal Law: Cases and Materials*. Durham, N.C.: Carolina Academic Press, 2001.

Wynn, William J. *It's the Law: Pets, Animals and the Law*. Irvine, Calif.: Doral Publishing, 2001.

PET PHOTOGRAPHER

Allen, Larry. *Creative Canine Photography*. New York: Allworth Press, 2003.

Nichols, Ron. *How to Take Great Pet Pictures: Recipes For Outstanding Results With Any Camera*. Buffalo, N.Y.: Amherst Media Inc., 2002.

PET PSYCHIC

Gurney, Carol. *The Beginner's Guide to Animal Communication: How to Listen and Talk With Your Animal Friend*. Louisville, Colo.: Sounds True, 2003.

McGillivray, Debbie, and Eve Adamson. *Complete Idiot's Guide to Pet Psychic Communication*. New York: Alpha Books/Penguin, 2004.

Williams, Marta. *Learning Their Language: Intuitive Communication with Animals and Nature*. Novato, Calif.: New World Library, 2003.

PET PSYCHOLOGIST

Dodman, Nicholas. *The Dog Who Loved Too Much: Tales, Treatments and the Psychology of Dogs*. New York: Bantam, 1997.

Lachman, Larry, and Frank Mickadiet. *Dogs on the Couch: Behavior Therapy for Training and Caring for Your Dog*. Woodstock, N.Y.: Overlook TP, 2002.

Wright, John C., and Judi Wright Lashnits. *The Dog Who Would Be King: Tales and Surprising Lessons from a Pet Psychologist*. Emmaus, Pa.: Rodale Press, 1999.

PET SITTER

Kimball, Cheryl. *Start Your Own Pet Sitting Business*. Irvine, Calif.: Entrepreneur Press, 2004.

Mangold, Lori. *The Professional Pet Sitter: Your Guide to Starting and Operating a Successful Service*. Central Point, Ore.: Paws-Itive Press, 2005.

Moran, Patti J. *Pet Sitting for Profit: A Complete Manual for Professional*

Success. New York: Howell Book House, 1997.

PETTING ZOO OPERATOR

Lock, Deborah. *Petting Zoo.* London: DK Readers, 2005.

Hanson, Elizabeth. *Animal Attractions: Nature on Display in American Zoos.* Princeton, N.J.: Princeton University Press, 2004.

PET WASTE REMOVAL SPECIALIST

Osborn, Matthew. *The Professional Pooper-Scooper: How to start your own low-cost, high-profit dog waste removal service.* Columbus, Ohio: Matthew Osborn, 1999.

SHEEP SHEARER

Cardell, Kim. *Practical Sheep Keeping.* Wiltshire, United Kingdom: Crowood Press, 1998.

Parker, Ron. *The Sheep Book: A Handbook for the Modern Shepherd.* Chicago: Swallow Press, 2001.

WILDLIFE REHABILITATOR

Jacobs, Shannon. *Healers of the Wild: Rehabilitating Injured and Orphaned Wildlife.* Boulder, Colo.: Johnson Books, 2003.

Ruth, Irene. *First Aid for Wildlife: Basic Care for Birds and Mammals.* Brandford, Conn.: Bick Publishing House, 1997.

ZOOKEEPER

Liebman, Dan. *I Want to Be a Zookeeper.* Buffalo, N.Y.: Firefly Books, 2003.

Space, Lori Day. *The Zookeeper's Daughter.* Frederick, Md.: PublishAmerica, 2004.

INDEX

Page numbers in **bold** indicate major treatment of a topic.

A

Academy of Equine Dentistry, The 45
AFA. *See* American Farriers Association (AFA)
AKC. *See* American Kennel Club
AKC Gazette 39
American Association of Laboratory Animal Scientists 48
American Association of Zoo Veterinarians 48
American Boarding Kennels Association 12, 23
American Farriers Association (AFA) 51
American Humane Association 11, 12
American Humane Society 88
American Institute for Animal Science 12, 23
American Kennel Club 25, 35, 37–39
American Sign Language (ASL) 21
American Veterinary Medical Association (AVMA) 48, 59
Animal Behavior Associates 3
animal behaviorist **1–4**, 109
animal communicators 82–84
animal coordinator 12–16
animal forensic specialist **5–8**, 109

Animal Planet 10
Animal Precinct (TV series) 10
animal shelter director **9–11**, 109–110
animal wrangler **12–16**, 110–111
Anne (Princess) 85
aquarist **17–18**, 111
Ashland laboratory 6
ASL. *See* American Sign Language (ASL)
ASPCA Humane Law Enforcement Department (New York City) 10
assistance dog trainer **19–22**, 111–112
Association for Primate Veterinarians 48
associations, organizations, and Web sites x–xi, 109–127. *See also under specific topics*
Audubon Zoo 103
AVMA. *See* American Veterinary Medical Association (AVMA)

B

Bide-A-Wee Home 75
Bronx Zoo 106
Bucks County Animal Rescue League 10

C

Camp Bow Wow 27
Canadian Kennel Club 37
Canine Companions for Independence 21
career tests and inventories 136

Carey, Mariah 73
Central Michigan University 7
CITIES. *See* United National Convention on International Trade in Endangered Species (CITIES)
Colorado State University 3
Council on Education of the American Veterinary Association 48, 59

D

Daktari (TV show) 13
Dallas Morning News 25
DBA papers. *See* "Doing Business As" papers
Department of Agriculture (USDA). *See* United States Department of Agriculture (USDA)
Doctor of Veterinary Medicine 47, 48, 59
dog day care owner **23–27**, 113
D.O.G. Development 27
dog groomer **28–31**, 113–114
dog handler **32–35**, 114
dog show judge **36–40**, 114
"Doing Business As" papers 14, 23, 28, 32, 52
DoodyCalls 96–97
dude rancher **41–43**, 115
Dude Ranchers Association 43
D.V.M. *See* Doctor of Veterinary Medicine

E

Endangered Species Act of 1973 5
equine dentist **44–46,** 115–116
exotic animal veterinarian **47–50,** 116–117

F

farrier **51–55,** 117–118
Florida, University of College of Veterinary Medicine 61

G

general careers 136
Gentle Ben (TV show) 13
gourmet dog treat baker **56–58,** 118
Graduate Record Examination (GRE) 63
Great Dog Bakery 57
Guide Dogs for the Blind 22
guide dog trainer. *See* assistance dog trainer
Guiding Eyes 21

H

Happy Paws Pet Sitting 90
Hartsdale Pet Cemetery 73, 75
High-Stone Pet Lodge 25–26
holistic veterinarian **59–63,** 119
Holistic Veterinary Center 61
horseshoeing. *See* farrier
horse whisperer **64–66,** 119
Humane Society of the United States 11, 12, 23

I

Iditarod Trail Sled Dog Race 70
International Veterinary Acupuncture Society (IVAS) 61, 62
International Wildlife Rehabilitation Council 102
IVAS. *See* International Veterinary Acupuncture Society (IVAS)

J

Johnson, Samuel 73

K

Kansas State University 49

L

Law School Admission Test (LSAT) 78

M

marine mammal trainer **67–69,** 120
Marine World 13, 69
Maryland, University of 12
Medical College Admission Test (MCAT) 63
Merrill, Robert 73
Mi-Sha-Oak kennels 37
Missouri, University of 10
Mohawk College 37
Moorpark College 15
Mountain Mushers, Inc. 71
Multistate Bar Examination (MBE) 77
musher **70–72,** 120–121

N

NASCAR 93
National Animal Control Association 11, 12, 23

National Dog Groomers Association of America 29
National Holistic Veterinary Medical Association 60
National Park Service 6
National Professional Pet Sitters Association 88
National Wildlife Rehabilitators Association 102
New Secrets of Successful Dog Show Handling (Green and Migliorini) 34
New York Aquarium 18
New York School of Dog Grooming 30

O

Occupational Outlook Handbook ix, x
Oklahoma Horseshoeing School 43
online career resources xi, 129–136
  career tests and inventories 136
  search engines 129–130
  Web sites 130–135

P

Pennsylvania, University of Behavior Clinic of Veterinary Hospital 86
pet cemetery owner **73–75,** 121
pet lawyer **76–78,** 122
pet photographer **79–81,** 122–123
pet psychic **82–84,** 123
pet psychologist **85–87,** 123–124
Pet Rest Gardens 74
pet sitter **88–91,** 124

Pet Sitters International 88, 90

petting zoo operator **92–94,** 124–125

pet waste removal specialist **95–98,** 125

Philadelphia Inquirer 86

Poop VanScoop 98

R

Rhode Island, University of 106

Ross, Diana 73

S

School of Culinary Arts 57

Schrever, Stewart 73

search engines 129–130

Secondhand Lions 13

Seeing Eye dogs. *See* assistance dog trainer

September 11, 2001 terrorist attack 90

sheep shearer **99–101,** 125

Sheep Shearers, Inc. 100

Smith, Kate 73

Sprucedale 42

Spy Kids 13

Sunday Delaware News Journal 86

Sunrise Exotic Ranch 14

U

United National Convention on International Trade in Endangered Species (CITIES) 5

United States Department of Agriculture (USDA) 92, 93

U.S. Bureau of Labor Statistics ix

USDA. *See* United States Department of Agriculture (USDA)

U.S. Department of Labor 9

U.S. Fish and Wildlife Service 6

V

Veterinary College Admission Test (VCAT) 63

Veterinary Teaching Hospital, Colorado State University 3

Virginia-Maryland Regional College of Veterinary Medicine 12

Voith, Victoria 86

W

Web sites 130–135

Westminster dog show 33, 34

wildlife rehabilitator **102–104,** 125–127

Wildlife Rescue and Rehabilitation 103

World Trade Center September 11, 2001 terrorist attack 90

Z

zookeeper **105–107,** 127